The One-Room Schoolhouse

The One-Room Schoolhouse

Paul Rocheleau

Foreword by Verlyn Klinkenborg

UNIVERSE

MISSION RIDGE SCHOOL
Donated by:
Mason County Extension
Homemakers
Ridge School stands as memorial at farm museum
0123456789

First published in the United States of America in 2003 by UNIVERSE PUBLISHING

A Division of Rizzoli International Publications, Inc., 300 Park Avenue South, New York, NY 10010, www.rizzoliusa.com

©2003 Universe Publishing

2003 2004 2005 2006 2007 / 10 9 8 7 6 5 4 3 2 1

All photographs ©Paul Rocheleau, except for spine photograph: ©Getty Images, ED000750

Printed in the United States of America

Design by Claudia Brandenburg

ISBN: 0-7893-1001-5

Library of Congress Catalog Control Number: 2003104950

Foreword

by

Verlyn Klinkenborg

Consider yourself lucky if you come across a one-room country schoolhouse. Like a colonnade of mature elms along a village street or a covered bridge over a narrow river or a lighthouse on an Atlantic headland, the one-room schoolhouse belongs to a more fortunate if almost forgotten landscape. If you find one now, especially in the Midwest, it's likely to be standing alone, curiously detached from what lies around it. The rows of corn and soybeans come to an abrupt end at a careful patch of lawn surrounding a small white building that retains its formality, no matter how weather-beaten the roof and siding have become. On a spring day, before the crops have risen very high, a schoolhouse like that seems to stand alone in an empty world. Where the children would have come from to fill even that one bare room is not apparent.

But there was a time, in my parents' generation, when a one-room schoolhouse—almost chapel-like in its demeanor—rose like a buoy of learning in a sea of ignorance. The townships were full of small farms then, and the farms were full of children. Town itself was still strictly a Saturday affair, a place to go to market, to exchange gossip, to begin the spending, in imagination at least, of one's hard-won childhood earnings. The idea of going there every day to school would have seemed very strange, a squandering of all that excitement on the day-to-day business of learning your letters. It was hard to argue with the practicality of a schoolhouse down at the pasture end of the road, set in the midst of the workaday landscape, and yet slightly apart. You can almost picture a bird's-eye view of the scene, perhaps on a fall day when the corn is ripe, children trudging down the gravel roads, exploring the ditches, cutting through a slack fence here and there, until they all converge on the schoolhouse, brothers, sisters, cousins, neighbors.

Perhaps this sounds nostalgic or merely antiquarian, however, the idea was to distribute education in a way that made it convenient to the children, instead of distributing children in a way that made it convenient to the schools. But there were other ideas associated with those schoolhouses, too. In one room, there was space for only one teacher, one salaried teacher, that is. Yet nearly everyone who ever attended a one-room schoolhouse will tell you that the students themselves turned into teachers. There was no room to segregate grades, so the older and the younger children mingled, bound not only by proximity but also, often, by kinship. The world of a schoolhouse like that was small enough to make even a shy child feel like there was a possibility of conquering it. Compared to a crowded, jostling modern school, a one-room schoolhouse lacked many things. But what it lacked was also, in many cases, what it had to offer.

Consolidation killed those old schoolhouses. The farms got bigger and bigger and the number of people living in the countryside got fewer and fewer. Children began to make a daily trek into town to school, and over time even those town schools began to consolidate as the rural population continued to dwindle, until it took two or three towns to fill a grade school. To a younger generation, like mine, the one-room schoolhouses standing at a crossroads became matters of mere curiosity. The thought of going to school in one seemed as strange as the thought of driving a Model A Ford. But to an older generation, the Ford and the schoolhouse seem as natural as memories always do.

I know that what strikes me now about those buildings is the peace that surrounds them. It hardly matters where you come across them, in Montana or Wyoming or Iowa or farther east. Park your car across the road or, better yet, a little farther up the right-of-way where you can't see it. When you reach the schoolhouse step onto the school ground. You can imagine, if you like, the sound of farm kids, so raucous and yet so modest, playing at noon, as if they were part of a Winslow Homer painting. But it's no less gratifying just to listen to the sound of what's there instead of the sound of what used to be. It may be the wind across the corn tassels or the oats. It may be the clink of a chain against a flagpole. It may be the sound of a grain truck some distance down the road or even, if you're very lucky, the low sound of cattle quartered under the shade in a nearby pasture. The very silence of the afternoon itself could be the sound of empty farmland, where humans are now so few, or it could be just the sound of after-school, when the books have been put away and all those kids have gone home to do chores.

Introduction

by

Paul Rocheleau

I was first exposed to one-room schoolhouses in 1988 when I was commissioned to photograph the Smithsonian Institution's New England guidebooks on historical America. There was an air about these old structures that I found enchanting. Maybe what so inspired me were the spirits of the long-departed teachers holding court in the front of the room, sometimes friendly, sometimes stern, or perhaps the thoughts of the adorable little pupils enthusiastically raising their hands to the teachers or wriggling about in their seats anxiously awaiting recess. I knew immediately there was potential for a book. The idea, however, remained dormant until three years ago. It sprang back to life when, while working on a book of the Berkshires, I photographed my town's newly restored one-room schoolhouse. Thoughts of how to pursue it swelled in my head. I knew the time had come to make my move.

Before starting this book, I knew I had to be concise about my subject, determine how to approach its presentation, and identify my audience. By exploring previous books on the subject I knew what I did not want to do. As a visually oriented person, not a scholar of my subject, I wanted to appeal to an interested general public, one that would be apt to understand the need for preservation. I chose to present the topic as a full-color photographic essay with text that would be journalistic in approach. I wanted to maintain a contemporary attitude so that my readers might experience the subject matter as I did—hence, the reason for modern-day color photographs as opposed to historical imagery. Back in the heyday of the one-room schoolhouse, when photographs of the teachers and students were taken, the long exposures necessitated a very still pose, which falsely made the subjects look grim. Young children are not grim. When artists of the era depicted the schools they usually showed some hijinks going on in the room or outside.

For this project, I planned to visit all forty-eight contiguous states (my odometer clocked more than 25,000 miles) and wrote to each state's historical office to ask for their suggestions for schools they deemed worthy of recognition. With their aid, with word-of-mouth tips from friends and strangers, and by pure serendipity, the schoolhouses in this book were weeded out of thousands of structures still remaining. As for Alaska and Hawaii, I dreamed of adding the former, and my wife dreamed of accompanying me to the latter, but budgets on these projects do have limits.

In any journalistic endeavor there are restrictions to word count, even more so for books that are illustrated. As a photographer I never gave the text of a book much thought, or probably sympathy. But on this project I decided to take on the writing chore myself, as that would best express my personal experience and findings, something no outside writer could achieve without witnessing the subject first-hand. Thus I tried to keep the text at a fair length, making sure to provide enough necessary information of fact and experience that would fully complement a photographic book.

This book is dedicated to all the teachers who have stood in front of a classroom and, in love of their profession, gave of themselves tirelessly in enlightening their pupils to all the wonders of the world. One of those teachers was my now retired brother Guy Rocheleau. Art took on another dimension in his junior high classes. **P.R.**

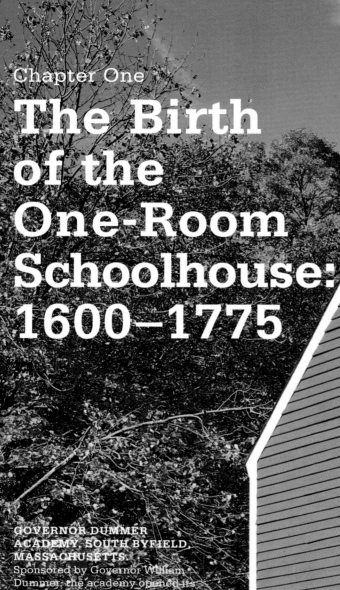

Chapter One

The Birth of the One-Room Schoolhouse: 1600–1775

GOVERNOR DUMMER ACADEMY, SOUTH BYFIELD, MASSACHUSETTS. Sponsored by Governor William Dummer, the academy opened its doors to twenty-eight students on March 1, 1773, with Samuel Moody as master. The academy has been in continuous operation to this day, making it the oldest in the country.

Every year during the week leading up to Thanksgiving, a flurry of activity takes place across the United States among grammar school students. Little students busy at work over their desks and tables enthusiastically cut out and color representations of Pilgrims, Native Americans, and turkeys. Some may dress up as Pilgrims and Indians, practicing for the annual school play that proud camcorder-toting parents eagerly await. The important lesson from all this activity—to give thanks—is etched into impressionable minds as students learn about the trials and tribulations of the Pilgrims' first year. However, something very immediate to those children is usually ignored during these Thanksgiving rituals: to give thanks due to the Pilgrims and Puritans of New England for having been the primary influence in the development of American education as we practice it today.

New England culture was not the only influence upon the American scholastic model. Along the eastern seaboard, the middle and southern colonies also contributed to the present system of public education. What was happening in those early one-room schools that made the American system of education different from its antecedents in Europe?

Similarities with European educational systems did exist. Prior to the colonization of America, education was firmly established on the European continent. In its early history there, the only recipients were the clergy and aristocracy, with the rest of society learning by apprenticeship or remaining illiterate. With Johannes Gutenberg's invention of the movable-type printing press in the mid-fifteenth century, knowledge began to diffuse and circulate out to the general population. After the Protestant Reformation, the clergy of certain sects encouraged their congregations to read the Bible, especially after it had been translated from Greek and Latin into the vernacular languages of Europe. What a stimulus this was for making society more literate! During the fifteenth to eighteenth centuries more specialized professions developed within society, some by technical innovations in the production of goods, others by the explosion of mercantilism throughout the world. The increasingly sophisticated cultures became aware of the need to school most children in the basics of reading, writing—and beyond, for the intelligent child. Those ideals and abilities crossed the Atlantic with the immigrant leaders and their followers as they colonized the strange New World.

Joining the English Puritans in New England were the Dutch and French Huguenots in New York, the Quakers in New Jersey and Pennsylvania, and English Anglicans in Virginia, Georgia, and the Carolinas, with other ethnic European groups scattered throughout the Americas. All of them were trying to find their own little plots of the new Eden, which made for a highly diverse and interesting mix of people. The one aspect that granted some sense of unity was that most settlers were Protestant. Granted, there had been some very early groups of Jewish immigrants in Rhode Island and New York, and through a land grant given to a Catholic Englishman, the Earl of Baltimore, Maryland had a fair-sized, if not majority, group of Catholic immigrants. All in all, though, the thirteen colonies comprised a "Protestant nation," with each denomination placing an emphasis on schools to indoctrinate its children with the teachings of the prevailing church.

JAMESTOWN, SETTLEMENT, JAMESTOWN, VIRGINIA.
A replica of the English settlement in the years 1610–14.

Today, most religions cleave into orthodox, conservative, and liberal factions, which was also the case in the American colonies. In the most simple terms—as Colonial religion was so fraught with nuances there is not enough space here to thoroughly delve into it—the northern colonies tended toward orthodox Protestant practice, the middle colonies, while not necessarily "liberal," for practical reasons leaned toward tolerance, while in the Southern colonies conservatism mirrored the religions "back home in England." These patterns had a direct effect on each region's educational patterns.

The orthodox outlook of the New England Puritans called for their religion to permeate their entire Colonial culture. According to their doctrine, every congregation member had to be able to read and discuss the Bible. They believed that personal salvation was connected with understanding the Bible's teachings, and that if you could not relate to the words of the Lord, then your chance for salvation was severely hindered. For this reason, the Massachusetts Bay Colony became the first of the colonies to enact regionwide laws making it mandatory to provide reading and writing instruction to the children of each community.

Though prior to the nation's separation of church and state these laws initially followed a sectarian agenda, their enactment by the General Court of Massachusetts, which had jurisdiction over the whole colony, provided the foundation for the concept that education may be governed by the laws of the state governments. The first law in 1642 established the need to teach the children "as may enable them perfectly to read the English tongue, and [gain] knowledge of the capitol laws: upon penalty of twenty shillings for each neglect therein." The next law, in 1647, established the need for structural space and teachers: "... after the Lord hath increased them to the number of fifty householders, shall then forthwith appoint one within their towns to teach all such children as shall resort to him to write and read, whose wages shall be paid either by the parents or masters of such children or by the inhabitants in general." In communities of more than 100, they were to "set up a grammar school to instruct youth [boys] so far as they may be fitted for the university."

This was all well and good in terms of the principles of publicly financed education, but as can be seen in today's world, where edicts seem to flow like rivers from state and federal agencies, how much of this really was implemented depended both on the commitment of the community towards education and on its financial strength. In a book published in 1834 on the history of the Massachusetts towns of Ipswich, Essex, and Hamilton, author Joseph B. Felt lists the actual state of literacy in the 1760s: "Three quarters of a century back, a large part of the wills left by men, some of whom had considerable property, were signed with a cross. This remark was still more applicable to the wills of females, though some of them were wealthy and respectable. Such facts were not peculiar to the people of Ipswich. They existed in all sections of our country."

In the middle colonies and Rhode Island we find that religion also influenced education. In 1636 Roger Williams, a Puritan dissident of liberal leanings, left Massachusetts with a flock of believers to start the Rhode Island colony. In practicing tolerance, the colony became open to different ideas and religions. In New York City, the Dutch colony was tolerant of diversity for practical reasons: trade and business, which brought a diversified population to the isle of Manhattan, was central to their livelihood. New Jersey and Pennsylvania, with their liberal Quaker population, also followed in this vein, but were more intent on keeping their territories Quaker. Pennsylvania was such a large colony that other denominations, especially the German sects of Moravians and Mennonites, took the opportunity to settle west of the Quaker settlements. Even further west were the Scots-Irish of the Presbyterian church. In all, the educational systems in these colonies followed a development path similar to that of Massachusetts, but with a twist. Whereas Massachusetts, Connecticut, and New Hampshire were able to dictate their education laws to the whole colony because of the Puritan monopoly, the middle colonies, with their greater diversity, could not come up with a consensus for colony-wide education laws. Every sectarian faction thought the others would benefit by imposing their religious ideas where they were not wanted. So instead of being colonywide, education laws became fractionalized to the territory of each religious community.

In the southern colonies, where the conservative Anglican Church held sway, the educational system was quite similar to England's. The problem that arose in the southern colonies was the expansion of land acreage from generation to generation as farms turned into plantations. With fewer areas of population concentration, public education was harder to implement. Education laws that had been passed for establishment of parish school districts and curriculums, some of which were very innovative—even addressing the advanced schooling of girls—did not fare as well in implementation as in the northern colonies. Many of the large tidewater landowners—in North Carolina, Virginia, and Maryland—sent their children overseas to school in England. Since these families had great influence within each colony, the

practice did not bode well for establishing a viable general public education system, though public education did take place.

Similar types of education were available for children throughout the colonies because of either the commonality of their English heritage or their roots in Protestant religion. The simplest method of education and probably the most used in frontier areas was home schooling. Of course, this was contingent on one or two of the parents being literate enough to provide instruction. As settlements grew on the frontier, the prevailing laws in most colonies required having an elementary school for the basics of reading, along with instruction in such fields as writing, religion, and basic colonial law, as Massachusetts did in 1647. Girls might have received additional lessons in sewing, weaving, and other home arts. A child who was going to progress to the secondary level would spend only two to three years in elementary education. Those who were not going to continue—in the beginning, all girls did not— would stay in the elementary school until they were between ten and twelve. "Dame schools" were another option: a woman of some literacy and character, usually a widow, would take in the local children for a fee or in barter, and teach them fundamentals. These women probably were born to professional families who valued education and made sure to educate their daughters as well as their sons. While wealthy upper-class parents could hire tutors to come into the home to teach their children, apprenticeships were an important means of preparing youth of lesser status for a productive adulthood. An apprenticeship contract agreed that a child would be indentured for a specific period of time to learn the trade of a master.

During this time the master would provide for the boy or girl as if for his own child and, according to laws usually in place by the colonies, was responsible for his or her schooling in the areas of reading, writing, and religion.

Provision was also made in the colonies to prepare exceptional students for entry into schools of higher learning through enrollment in secondary schools. Sometimes called English free schools—free to those who were poor but funded by taxing the community's residents—and based on the English academic system, these schools were known as "Latin grammar schools." On the European continent and in the colonies, colleges taught most of their material in the original language of ancient scholars: Latin, Greek, and sometimes Hebrew. To gain acceptance into any college, it was mandatory to have command of Latin and some Greek, hence the term "Latin grammar school." For those who could afford it, there were private academies that also prepared boys (girls were not expected to go to college) for higher schools of learning. Some of those academies were endowed enough to offer further education to especially bright poor children who could not pay the tuition. One such institution that still exists is the Governor Dummer Academy in Byfield, Massachusetts.

Around the middle of the eighteenth century, complaints grew about this classical form of secondary education. The Latin grammar school was becoming an antiquated concept as the colonies were becoming more modernized, civilized, and prosperous. In 1749, Benjamin Franklin proposed an academy that would

Jamestown Settlement Church, Jamestown, Virginia. The settlement's church was constructed of wattle-and-daub walls and a thatched roof. A church would have also been used as a schoolhouse in early settlements.

teach subjects in business, technology, sciences, mathematics, and other disciplines that were of practical value for the dynamic growth that was taking place in the colonies. The curriculum would be chosen according to the vocation each student wanted to pursue. Franklin, though, was ahead of his time and perhaps somewhat too secular with his ideas; classicists and their religious allies would hold sway with their system for some time.

To give a feeling of an actual one-room schoolhouse in session during the Colonial period, I offer the following snippets from a wonderful treatise on the subject by Christopher Dock, a Mennonite schoolmaster who taught in Pennsylvania in the middle to late 1700s. Dock's dedication to teaching and to the students is evident in his words, and even though some forms of discipline may sound harsh to contemporary ears, his good intent to steer young souls towards moral, responsible adulthood is pervasive.

On the start of the school day, Dock states: "The children arrive as they do because some have a great distance to school, others a short distance, so that the children cannot assemble as punctually as they can in a city. Therefore, when a few children are present, those who can read their Testament sit together on one bench; but the boys and girls occupy separate benches .... When all are together, and examined, whether they are washed and combed, they sing a psalm or a morning hymn, and I sing and pray with them. As much as they can understand of the Lord's prayer and the ten commandments...."

On being a new student and its rewards: "... the child is first given a welcome by the other children, who extend their hands to him. Then I ask him if he will be diligent and obedient. If he promises this, he is

told how to behave; and when he can say his A B C's...
[here Dock brings in the child's parents for positive
reinforcement] his father owes him a penny, and his
mother must fry him two eggs."

If a student was not diligent Dock would resort
to peer pressure: "... any one having failed in more
than three trials a second time [the second set of
three attempts to get it right] is called 'Lazy' by the
entire class and his name is written down. Whether
such a child feared the rod or not, I know from experience that this denunciation by the children hurts
more than if I were constantly to wield and flourish
the rod." Further thoughts about corporal punishment: "Experience teaches that a timid child is
harmed rather than benefited by harsh words or
much application of the rod, and to improve it, other
means must be employed. Likewise a stupid child is
only harmed. A child that is treated to too much flog-
ging at home is not benefited by it at school, but it is
made still worse."

Turning his thoughts away from punishment and
on to social rewards, Dock states: "But when I find
that the little ones are good enough at their reading to
be fit to read the Testament, I offer them to good
Testament readers for instruction [older students].
The willing teacher takes the pupil by the hand and
leads him to his seat."

Dock acknowledges that there are certain necessary problems to deal with that do not involve school-
work. When nature calls: "It is also noted that children
find it necessary to ask to leave the room, and one
must permit them to do this, not wishing the unclean-
ness and odor in the school. But the clamor to go out
would continue all day, and sometimes without need,
so that occasionally two or three are out at the same
time, playing. To prevent this I have driven a nail in

**NATHAN HALE SCHOOL, EAST
HADDAM, CONNECTICUT.**
Nathan Hale (famous for
his quotation, "I only regret
that I have but one life to give
to my country") taught at the
school from October 1773 to
1774. Moved to its present site
in 1899, the schoolhouse
has a commanding view of the
Connecticut River.

the door-post, on which hangs a wooden tag. Any one needing to leave the room looks for the tag."

His thoughts on how to handle aggression between students: "When children become angered at school or on the way there, and it is shown that both combatants are wrong, each one's fault is pointed out and the punishment for each defined, and also meted out if they are unwilling to make peace. Thereupon they are placed together on the punishment seat, apart from the other children until they are willing to make up; if not, deserved punishment will follow. But it rarely happens that they are put on the punishment seat. They prefer shaking hands, and then the case is adjusted. If this were the case among adults, and if they were as willing to forgive and forget, 'By lawsuits no purses depleted would be, And lawyers would never wax rich on their fee. Gnawing conscience would come to rest, With love and peace life would be blest; Much less of ache and dole, For heart and soul.'"

To sum up his overall feelings about his students and on teaching: "Regarding my friend's question, how I treat the children with love that they both love and fear me, I will say that in this respect I cannot take the least credit upon myself, if I am at all successful with children, either in teaching or in performing religious duties. First, I owe God particular thanks, because besides calling me to this profession He has given me an extreme love of children. For if it were not for love it would be an unbearable burden to live among children. But love bears and never tires."

Christopher Dock's words recall common experiences all of us have faced in school. Overwhelmingly teachers are dedicated, compassionate, and personable, with "bad and mean teachers" the exception. Good teachers, though, see their charges as individuals who sometimes need individual attention to bring

NATHAN HALE SCHOOL, EAST HADDAM, CONNECTICUT. The school interior offers some idea of the spartan seating and writing facilities that existed in the eighteenth century.

out the inherent talent that resides in all of us. Though we cannot be certain, this was probably the same during the stricter Colonial times as well. The understanding and sympathy for our past teachers becomes more acute as we mature and see in retrospect the grief that we gave these people in our youth with petulance and sassy ways. This understanding should carry through to the unique situations that existed in Colonial schools.

To further this thought, I offer the diary entry of John Adams of March 15, 1756, written in Worcester, Massachusetts, during his first year of teaching after graduation from Harvard:

"I sometimes, in my sprightly moments, consider my self, in my great Chair at School, as some Dictator at the head of a commonwealth. In this little State I can discover all the great Genius's, all the surprising actions and revolutions of the great World in miniature. I have severall renowned Generalls but 3 feet high, and several deep projecting Politicians in peticoats. I have others catching and dissecting Flies, accumulating remarkable pebbles, cockle shells &c., with as ardent Curiosity as any Virtuoso in the royal society. Some rattle and Thunder out A, B, C, with as much Fire and impetuosity, as Alexander fought, and very often sit down and cry as heartily, upon being out spelt, as Cesar did, when at Alexanders sepulchre he recollected that the Macedonian Hero had conquered the World before his Age. At one Table sits Mr. Insipid fopping and fluttering, spinning his whirligig, or playing with his fingers as gaily and wittily as any frenchified coxcomb brandishes his Cane or rattles his snuff box. At another sits the polemical Divind, plodding and wrangling in his mind about Adam's fall in which we sinned all as his primmer has it. In short my little school like the great World, is made up of Kings, Politicians, Divines, L.D., Fops, Buffoons, Fidlers, Sychophants, Fools, Coxcombs, chimney sweepers, and every other Character drawn in History or seen in the World. Is it not then the highest Pleasure my Friend to preside in this little World, to bestow the proper applause upon virtuous and generous Actions, to blame and punish every vicious and contracted Trick, to wear out of the tender mind every thing that is mean and little, and fire the new born soul with a noble ardor and Emulation. The World affords no greater Pleasure. Let others waste the bloom of Life, at the Card or biliard Table, among rakes and fools, and when their minds are sufficiently fretted with losses, and inflamed by Wine, ramble through the Streets, assaulting innocent People, breaking Windows or debauching young Girls. I envy not their exalted happiness. I had rather sit in school and consider which of my pupils will turn out in his future Life, a Hero, and which a rake, which a phylosopher, and which a parasite, than change breasts with them, tho possest of 20 lac'd wast coats and 1000 pounds a year."

John Adams soon left teaching to enter the law profession, and later began his illustrious career in government. His Worcester teaching must have had an impact, for in a letter to John Jebb dated September 10, 1785, he wrote, "The whole people must take upon themselves the education of the whole people, and must be willing to bear the expenses of it." The next era in education was to begin.

GOVERNOR DUMMER ACADEMY, SOUTH BYFIELD, MASSACHUSETTS.
View into the schoolroom showing tables and benches from the eighteenth century. The restoration was overseen by Perry, Shaw, and Hepburn of Boston, who also worked on the restoration projects in Colonial Williamsburg.

GOVERNOR DUMMER ACADEMY, SOUTH BYFIELD, MASSACHUSETTS.
(Left) View to the front showing the teacher's upright desk.
(Right) Original brass door key and Samuel Moody's chair.

Chapter Two

The Evolution of the One-Room Schoolhouse: 1776–1889

LEXINGTON, MASSACHUSETTS.
Daniel Chester French's
Minuteman Statue on the
town green.

On the morning of April 19, 1775, "the shot heard 'round the world" was fired across Lexington Green. The tiny Massachusetts colony had aggressively challenged the mighty British Empire, and in a human moment, a flashing muzzle changed the New World into "the brave new world." The thirteen colonies, no more than 155 years old, were thrust forward on an evolutionary path to a distinct American character and government—with American education in tow.

Though the war would consume the country's attention for the next seven years, educational development was not stopped short. Out of the battle zones life continued, as it usually does during conflict, as long as the immediate area is not under attack. Since many battles took place at strategic military sites, the average citizen had little direct involvement with the fighting. What did have a detrimental effect on education was the loss of school hours for the children who had to pick up the labor slack at home when their fathers and older brothers left their jobs for military duty.

The era showed progressive educational development when the second Continental Congress encouraged the newly formed states to develop their own constitutions. Many of these stipulated the need for public education and its financial support. As an example, Thomas Jefferson introduced a bill to the Virginia assembly in 1779 outlining in detail the public-education ideal in three steps: the establishment of a primary system, teaching the fundamentals of reading, writing, and mathematics for all children; the development of grammar schools to teach a higher level of the basics, namely, the sciences, higher mathematics, and classical languages; and for the most talented students, the introduction of classes at William and Mary

BRICK SCHOOL, WARREN, CONNECTICUT.
Built in the latter part of the eighteenth century, the Brick School had the distinction of being the longest continuously used one-room schoolhouse in the state.

College. Though his proposal was inspired by the school systems of Massachusetts, Connecticut, and New Hampshire, his ideas were more secular than what actually existed in those Puritan colonies. They included the teaching of Greek, Roman, and American history in place of the Bible's religious stories. His ideas were ahead of his time, and the Virginia legislature accepted only a small portion of his proposal. The bill, nonetheless, was prophetic as to what would take place nationally, especially after he assumed the presidency.

With independence established in 1782, the country was able to focus on developing a distinctively American style of education, apart from that of the European continent. One distinctive educational concept (and one that led to the proliferation of one-room schoolhouses) was the separation of townships into school districts. The original reason for this started before the Revolution, when territories became safe enough from Native American warfare to populate the outer fringes of townships. In contrast to Europe, where people lived in towns and went out in the mornings to farms in the country, Americans homesteaded the land, living where they farmed. Tension between farmers and town folks arose because of differing needs and life philosophies. Compounding those differences were children's needs for easy accessibility to a school. Whereas today there is the convenience of yellow school buses, no transportation system was then available for children except their little legs, and most town fathers did not want children to have to walk any farther than three miles to get to school. This meant that individual one-room schools had to be dotted throughout each township.

With the different needs and lifestyles between the people in the town and those in the hinterlands, conflict always existed between the groups regarding the type of education needed and how much money to allot for it. As a compromise they gave the responsibilities for taxing and maintaining a district school to each district's residential group. Central control for education in a township or a county was not to take place until later in the nineteenth to the middle of the twentieth century. Some effects of decentralization were the multitude of school architectural styles, differing educational curriculums, and varied budgets to meet each district's expectations for education.

Another Americanism was the vastness of land available for populating. The Treaty of Ghent transferred ownership of all land south of Canada to the United States, and the states ceded their western territorial claims to the new federal government. Twenty-some years following the Revolutionary War, the Louisiana Purchase almost doubled the territory claimed by the U.S. government. Both the state and federal governments began using land holdings as sources of great revenue by selling off tracts of land to developers for eventual sale to individual homesteaders. Before the sales could take place, however, most of the land had to be surveyed. In the new western territories the land was to be sectioned into six-square-mile townships and then further split into 36 square sections. Within townships, each one-sixteenth section (one square mile) was mandated by Congress to be used for the maintenance of schools. Monies derived from sales of land in the one-sixteenth section were to be used for construction of schools at ideal intervals of three miles, so all the town's children were within convenient walking distance to the structures.

Also influencing the development of education in the new nation was the separation of church and state. This had been in progress prior to the Revolution, but with the Declaration of Independence a separation of influence also took place between the mother churches of England and Europe and their Colonial offshoots (an exception being the Catholic church, which still was under the dictates of an English Catholic bishop and of the Vatican). The church administrations reorganized so that all matters of doctrine were dealt with in this country, and influenced by this country's unique needs and problems. On the rise were humanistic thought and philosophical ideologies such as Ralph Waldo Emerson's transcendental movement. Also, since differing Protestant denominations had to share the same geographical space, religions became less dogmatic. A live-and-let-live attitude prevailed except for the most ardent of believers. As a consequence, education became more a part of the public sector, with the understanding of the churches that the teaching of religious morals and doctrine was to take place in the house of worship on Sundays and at home, but not in the schools. Public education, with its general moral thought and more clearly academic curriculums, became an easier sell to the different denominations. They could see that no one religious thought was going to prevail over another in those influential thought centers, the schoolhouses. To work together in the common goal of children's education was to bring to the population an opportunity for education and knowledge previously unknown in the world.

"A popular Government, without popular information, or the means of acquiring it, is but a Prologue to a Farce or a Tragedy; or, perhaps both. Knowledge will forever govern ignorance. And a people who mean to be their own Governors, must arm themselves with the power which knowledge gives," wrote President James Madison to W. T. Hunt, on August 4, 1822. Madison was the fourth consecutive president to emphasize the importance of an educated public. Now with the declining influence on education of dogmatic religions, voices rose in all sectors of the population for a mandatory universal education system for the country—publicly funded and available for all students—called the common school. As with Jefferson's proposal to Virginia, the common-school idea was to bring a system of education to students from the earliest grades up to a public-funded state college. To thwart resistance from some elements of the religious community, the denominational religious schools and private academies were welcomed to continue and to be an important alternative to public education, but neither would receive public funds for their operation. The proponents of the "common" ideal hoped that not only the poor and middle class but also higher levels of society would send their children to common schools. It was such an American egalitarian ideal, an ideal that unbelievably did by and large become reality as the country matured.

What about female education? According to a section of the essay History of the Town of Hingham (1893):

"Early instruction in the art of reading was generally begun by the girls at home or in the numerous private schools taught by elderly women and known as the 'dame schools.' When they were sufficiently advanced, they were sent to the master, by whom they were taught to write, something of grammar, but rarely anything in geography or arithmetic. The girls' schools (there were five built separately from the boys' schools) were first established, not so much to give additional advantages in these branches as to give instruction in needle work and knitting, which useful branches of learning were outside of the qualifications of the master to teach." The order of instruction and

discipline in one of these schools has been described by one of its scholars: "The children were seated on benches around three sides of the room, the teacher occupying a position near the other side. The order of exercises was reading then sewing with an allotted task to complete before the close of the school which was ended with an exercise in spelling."

Education for girls continued to improve into the early nineteenth century when Horace Mann, an eloquent advocate of education reforms, and others of the common-school movement emphasized the need for female students to receive an education equal to that of the boys. A turning point for girls' education occurred in 1821 when Emma Willard started the Female Seminary in Troy, New York. It was the first institution of advanced learning for young women, a combination academy-college. The Troy Common Council appropriated $4,000 in tax revenues to fund its opening even though it was a private venture. They recognized the important mission the institution was going to provide for the higher education of young women. In its first year, Emma Willard had ninety students, of whom twenty-nine were from Troy and the others from as far away as Georgia, a response that reflected the growing desire in the country for equal opportunity for women in higher education. Another important milestone was marked at Oberlin College in Oberlin, Ohio, when it became the first college to introduce coeducational learning in 1833. In 1837, Mt. Holyoke College, another all-girls college, opened in Massachusetts. These were small but dramatic steps toward a serious approach to women's education. The opportunity given to women was returned tenfold to American education, when, beginning around the end of the century, young women graduating from all of the

BRICK SCHOOL, WARREN, CONNECTICUT.
Detail of an unusually patterned eight-over-eight window with original hardware on the shutter.

new coed and women's colleges became the primary pool for most teachers in the rapidly increasing numbers of one-room schools throughout the country.

Although American education indeed advanced through the nineteenth century, driven by less orthodoxy in religion, by a strong calling for a public-based education system, and by the advances of women's educational opportunities, the impression that educational reforms were proceeding without hurdles may be a bit misleading. Trying to get an accurate representation of education at that time is as hard as trying to give a concise description of a family of twelve with live-in grandparents. Each school in so many communities is on different levels of maturity, intelligence, and needs, along with differing personalities and reactions to any and all stimuli. Education throughout the nineteenth century was evolving, though at different paces in different regions. Certain areas of the country respected the need for education, others did not. Rural and frontier lands varied as to who was living on or immigrating to them. If the immigrants were from a European country that had high regard for education, or hailed from an eastern section of the country with similar ideas, then that particular area would prosper educationally. Such success reflected the most important part of good schooling, the parents and the parental community. Their involvement dictated the quality of teachers hired, the amount spent on the buildings and supplies, and the encouragement given to their own children and to those of their neighbors and relatives. (When you come to think about it, that pattern remains the same today.) A few examples of such parental influence: First, school attendance, while being mandatory, still suffered from lack of cooperation from parents who thought "book learnin'" was a waste of time. Ignorance was passed down from generation to generation, especially in sections of the country that already had a sketchy history of schooling. Larger cities took the lead in all educational reforms and development, with ideas diffusing out to the remote school sites. High schools, which started in Boston in 1821, had successfully spread through other East Coast cities and the upper Midwest. By 1860, their number had increased nationwide only to about 600; the common-school, universal-education concept still had not made converts of the wealthy and learned classes. Their choice of secondary education remained the private academy until around the very end of the century, when there were around 6,000 high schools and proportionally fewer academies.

As the country approached the end of the nineteenth century and the physical and mental wounds of the Civil War had begun to mend, the country went on a growth spurt that was enormous. From 1860 to 1920 the population grew from 30 million to 100 million, due mainly to a massive immigration of the world's peoples seeking relief and opportunity in a welcoming land. Many had heard of the Homestead Act of 1862 in their native lands. The act allowed individuals and families to claim 160 acres of potential farmland in the western territories. Starting in 1869, the government granted railroads land allotments as incentive to spur investment in railroad stock in order to fund a transportation infrastructure to enable rail travel across and around the nation. The railroads received land not only for their rights-of-way, but also acreage on both sides of the track to sell to potential farmers and ranchers. Thus, new agricultural entities provided the railroad with immediate customers who would ship their products with the railroads to the coastal markets.

All this activity created social needs that the federal and state governments had to address. Of course, education was one of the most important of the government's responsibilities. By the end of the century, state governments across the country were now much more actively involved in mandating compulsory education for children. Ideas about education were thus emerging from an incubation period that had begun with the first settlers; by the turn of the century the American educational ideal was one that we would recognize in today's world. That is, it was a "laddering system," with primary education being the first eight years (or nine years if the school had a kindergarten); then followed by four years of secondary schooling in high school, and finishing with state colleges and universities, as established in most states, for those continuing into higher learning.

At the same time, America's world-power position was expanding, driven by a combination of extensive natural resources, a well thought-out and stable government, a can-do work ethic, a talented native population, and an open immigration policy that brought fresh ideas and expertise to the whole mix. As may be expected, many small towns grew into cities and their education systems reflected the urban sophistication with bigger multi-room schools. Larger towns with hard-to-access outer reaches, smaller towns with less central density, and rural areas all continued to make use of the one-room schoolhouse. This system would make sense until transportation transformed the whole country into a school-bus culture. Improvements and reforms of educational ideas and practices diffused more quickly to one-roomers than they had in the past, derived mostly from better-educated teachers who had graduated from state universities and from highly esteemed eastern colleges. Given the control that par-

ents had on education, the children of America in the early twentieth century were bound to receive a very good education in those one-room schoolhouses—more than ever before.

Thus started the glory days of the one-room schoolhouse, a time when these structures thrived and entered American iconography. It is from this period that most of the buildings and stories featured in this book are drawn.

BRICK SCHOOL, WARREN, CONNECTICUT.
(Left) Entrance hall with coat rack. A wall between the entrance and the schoolroom prevented some of the cold air from entering in the winter.
(Right) A mix of school furniture from several periods.

BRATTONSVILLE FEMALE SEMINARY, BRATTONSVILLE, SOUTH CAROLINA.
(Left) Sponsored by Dr. John Bratton in 1840 the academy was added to the south side of his father's 1769 home. It was typical of rich landowners in the South to provide for the education of their children and other well-to-do families in the area.
(Right) An interior view of the schoolroom.

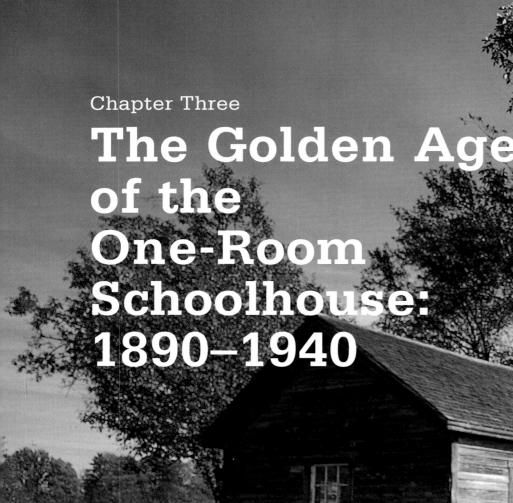

Chapter Three
The Golden Age of the One-Room Schoolhouse: 1890–1940

NEW LEBANON, NEW YORK.
A now privately owned
schoolhouse that has been left in
its natural state.

Mike Rakosnik
Present owner in front of the school he once attended,
Union School, District #31, DuBois, Nebraska.

" My land surrounded [the schoolhouse], and when it closed in 1963, I thought I could use it to store some of my farming equipment. Some boys who didn't like school would probably like to tear their old school down, so when I bought it, there was good-natured kidding in town about what my real reason for buying it was. But I had fun here, there were good times, and the teachers were pretty good."

It was a still blue morning in Nebraska on a day that was racing to become oppressively hot. The straight, though vertically undulating, dusty gravel road was leading me to the owner and former student of a unique schoolhouse. Built in 1923, the structure's architectural lines are pure Old World flourish, and tell of a group of immigrants that had come to make a new life for themselves, their children, relatives, and neighbors. All were Czechoslovakian. They, for some reason, had chosen this part of Nebraska in which to cluster, a natural phenomenon for immigrant groups. Clustering made the transition from Old World to New World so much easier when your neighbor could speak the same mother tongue— as well as the same tortured English.

The directions were excellent, and I had made good time. Such good time that I beat Mike Rakosnik's short drive to his schoolhouse. He pulled up soon enough, though, in a shiny, new, red four-seater Dodge pickup truck—the Great Plains equivalent to a yuppie's Porsche. He opened the door of the truck and let out a blast of cold air conditioning. He shook my hand with the power of someone who has worked hard during his life. Outfitted in bib overalls, a short-sleeve shirt, and a baseball cap, he was both very friendly and accommodating, though with a typical farmer's laconic conversational style. He had the key to open the front door and he suggested we go inside the school, partly to see the inside and partly to escape the hot sun—he had lost his tolerance for oppressive heat.

DUBOIS, NEBRASKA.
Czech social hall built in the same Old World style as the Union School, District #31. Both the school and the social hall had the same builder and reflected the importing of Eastern European building styles into the Midwest, where different ethnic groups immigrated en masse.

I asked him, as we entered the dark interior, how and why he got to purchase the schoolhouse. "My land surrounded it, and when it closed in 1963, I thought I could use it to store some of my farming equipment. Some boys who didn't like school would probably like to tear their old school down, so when I bought it, there was good-natured kidding in town about what my real reason for buying it was. But I had fun here, there were good times, and the teachers were pretty good."

The decaying big room was bare, so I had figured the classroom equipment had been sold or put in storage, but the sad response was that everything of value had been stolen over the years. This was not something I had expected to hear happen in a rural section of Nebraska. Rakosnik was 78 years old now, and if the building was going to be renovated it was going to have to survive till the next owner. We went outside to take some photographs.

The temperature was rising, especially in the sun. With the photography over, Rakosnik quickly suggested we go under the trees. "I can't stand the heat anymore," he said. Then he proceeded to tell me, "There used to be a school garden in this spot but a couple of boys tore it up. When the teacher found out who the culprits were, she made them plant these trees." We both praised the teacher's unknowing foresight to our immediate plight as the trees were now providing refuge from the scorching rays. I asked Rakosnik about other hijinks during his days and how the teacher coped. "Just run-of-the-mill stuff," he answered, "but in my father's days the teachers might have had it a bit tougher. In those days there was less mechanization on the farms, so the boys would be needed at home more. They sometimes wouldn't graduate 'til they were twenty. You could imagine they could be a handful, what with teenage girls to show off for." We talked for a short period more, then said goodbye. I took a few more pictures of the building, anxious to see the nearby Czech social hall, which Rakosnik said was erected around the same time by the same builder, and it had a very similar look. The hall had recently been renovated and placed on the National Register of Historic Places.

If there is one word that can be used to describe the architectural style of America's schoolhouses it would be vernacular—that is, "being the common building style of a period or place," as Merriam-Webster describes it. These structures were being put up by local craftspeople influenced by the styles of the period. So the look of the Czech school and social hall had as much validity to be called an American schoolhouse as the Mormon-built log schoolhouse I had visited in Fruita; the Wye Oak tidewater-style brick schoolhouse in Wye Mills, Maryland; the limestone schoolhouse in Marion County, Kansas; and all the others throughout the country.

The shapes of the buildings ran the gamut from square to round and everything in between. Why the builder or school committee would choose one style or shape is simply a matter of current fashion and

ALTAVILLE GRAMMAR SCHOOL, ALTAVILLE, CALIFORNIA. (Top left) One of the oldest schools in California, the 1858 school was erected with funds raised at a dance in a local saloon.

STERLING COUNTY SCHOOL #9, WING, NORTH DAKOTA. (Top right) This school also reflects immigrant architecture. In this part of the state, there was a strong German and Russian immigrant presence; not far away were Norwegian settlements.

CHOCCOLOCCO SCHOOL, CHOCCOLOCCO, ALABAMA. (Bottom left) Built in the 1880s, Choccolocco School was the school for the white children in town. It is due for restoration shortly.

DISTRICT #11, LEADVILLE, COLORADO. (Bottom right) A beautiful structure now owned by the school district that is used today to show present-day students the history of schooling in their town.

personal preference. Sometimes they would be influenced by a current idea of some expert as to what was the most efficient way to construct the buildings. In two types of instances, this expert opinion was found to be of fault. The hexagon- or octagon-shaped school was promoted as an encompassing design with the teacher in the center, and the students placed around the teacher's desk. It did not take long to find out that the teacher's back was going to be exposed to some classroom cutups. A lot of these were built, but this inherent flaw quickly sent the design into retirement. A second flawed design was one in which they placed windows just on the south and west sides of the buildings. They believed that with north-side windows, light would double-shadow the students' work area. As a photographer, I find this idea inconceivable, because north light is so soft that it only acts as a fill to the contrasting light that comes from south-side windows. And when you think that school sessions took place during the months of a low sun, having just south and west windows only worsened the contrasting lighting situation.

If I did not know this already, it was reinforced when I photographed at Sweet Briar School in early November. My first day was very bright and sunny. Inside were ceiling banks of fluorescent lights, which when used with bright sunlight, caused all types of filtering problems in my attempts to acquire normal color rendition on film (fluorescents give off a green cast). I decided to shut off the overheads and just use the natural light coming in from the south windows as would have happened in the schools out in the plains

OLD TUBAC SCHOOLHOUSE, TUBAC, ARIZONA.
Built in 1885, the early one-room, dirt-floored, adobe school also served as a church for priests coming in from Nogales to perform masses, funerals, baptisms, and weddings.

before they were electrified. The lighting was harsh on the children (as that school still holds classes), and I appreciated their patience with me as they worked under those conditions for the duration of the day.

One of the best lighting situations I saw, though, was at a Frank Lloyd Wright two-room schoolhouse in Wyoming Valley, Wisconsin, one of my five favorite Wright designs. Wright placed banks of floor-to-ceiling windows on the two exterior exposed sides of each classroom to bring in a flood of light, and also to have the children feel they were immersed within the landscape. That last idea was in contrast to earlier thoughts on window placement, where they felt the windows should be placed high so the students would not be distracted by the outdoors. Breaking the roof was a long, low-slung, windowed, cupola-style skylight, bringing in wonderful soft light to all the rooms.

Building-material choices for schoolhouses were not as varied as the choice of architectural design, though they still ran the gamut. The first schoolhouses that were erected in any locality were usually constructed of the most readily available material that the builders could handle. There might have been beautiful limestone lying just inches below the ground, but if the builders did not have the expertise to work with stone then they resorted to whatever could be used: sod, adobe brick (dried mud), or trees (logs). With time, as areas became prosperous, parents had the means to afford better buildings. Prosperity also brought in

FRUITA SCHOOLHOUSE, CAPITOL REEF NATIONAL PARK, UTAH.
Fruita Schoolhouse was built in 1896 by Mormon settlers in the Freemont River Valley. Because the settlement was quite remote, the log school stayed in use until 1941. During its heyday, the community would hold socials, dancing events, and Sunday school instruction in the school's small but cozy interior.

FAIRVIEW SCHOOL, GUNNISON COUNTY, COLORADO.
Nicely restored by the local residents, this school had a lovely porch
that gave it its own distinct look. Small architectural
embellishments gave schools very individualistic appearances.

FAIRVIEW SCHOOL

skilled tradesmen and buildings would be beautifully constructed from brick, stone, and sawed lumber over well-executed post-and-beam construction. If the state was doing well economically, the government would mandate specific architectural styles and building materials to be used in the construction of schools. Photo illustrations of the beautifully designed schoolhouses of the 1880s in Ohio and Indiana, with their elaborate brickwork, are a testament to their towns' very good economic times.

The architectural styles of schoolhouses did not always have education as their sole consideration. Schoolhouses sometimes played dual, or even triple, roles in a community. As one looks at the variety of schoolhouses, one can imagine that if a Christian cross were placed on top of the bell tower, it would indistinguishable from a church. In fact, some of them also served as worship spaces. If a community was all of the same religion then it made sense to consolidate the two functions into one space, such as the Mormon log church/schoolhouse in Torrey, Utah. A more prevailing second function was to use the school as a community center. This made good sense because the schools had been placed at strategic locations to facilitate an easy walk for children, so they became a convenient site for parents and other adults in the area to gather together. As a social hall, there were dances to be held, school plays to watch, and weddings to celebrate. As a town hall or local forum, it served the people as a place to solve district school matters, express their political ideas, take care of local problems, and cast the ballot to vote in the political saviors or to throw some "bums" out.

We cannot leave the sphere of architecture without bringing out from the background and up to the forefront the outhouse, otherwise called the necessary

OCTAGONAL SCHOOL, NEW CASTLE COUNTY, DELAWARE. (Below) This is a unique octagonal schoolhouse finished in stucco.
SODOM SCHOOLHOUSE, MILTON, PENNSYLVANIA. (Right) The octagonal Sodom Schoolhouse was built in 1814 of local stone, a widely used traditional building material in Pennsylvania.

(very polite word), the privy (also polite), and . . . oh, it is just too impolite. Whatever the outhouse was called, its primary purpose was to take care of nature's functions. However, it served three other purposes: as an escape from the classroom, especially when it was known that some question was about to be asked to which a student did not know the answer; a getaway for friends to enjoy unscheduled play time; and, for many a boy, to provide a vent for his mischief.

Concerning this third purpose, I heard a story from Larry Nelson at the Rock Hill School, in Oregon. The local teacher's four-year-old son would accompany his mother to school on occasion. As a four-year-old boy would, he was trying to make friends and hang out with the older boys. Several boys, playing on that desire, brought a can of green paint and a brush to school one morning. Out of sight of his mother, they asked the boy if he would like to be part of the group. "Yes," he said. "Well, we would like you to do us a favor that we don't have time to do." "Okay." "Teacher asked us to paint something, but we have to be in class shortly. After the bell goes off and we are all in the schoolhouse, go into the girls' privy and paint the seat with the fresh green paint. Then put the paint behind the bushes and we'll grab it on our way home." The irony of the story, after I asked what happened to those boys, was that the punishment went solely to the teacher's son. Flabbergasted, I asked why. "Ah," said Larry, "a teacher's child was like a parson's child, to be above reproach. His lesson had to be firmly learned."

DISTRICT'S #34 SCHOOL, CHASE COUNTY, KANSAS.
I came across an unexpected treat, in District's #34 School, built of native limestone in 1896. The two widely spaced privies, flanking the school, were also built of limestone.

MARION COUNTY, KANSAS. (Left)
I saw this abandoned school as I was driving on Route 150 and was drawn to its wonderful coloration and quirky front entrance.

LOWER FOX CREEK SCHOOL, STRONG CITY, KANSAS. (Top right)
The Lower Fox Creek School was built in 1882 on land donated by Steven F. Jones and stayed in operation until 1930. It was built of the same limestone that underlay its site on top of the knoll. It is now part of the Tallgrass Prairie National Preserve.

ROLLING GREEN, SOUTH DAKOTA. (Bottom right)
The school's name was probably just a district number; no date was etched into its skin and its closure was not recorded. But, as I stood in the endless prairie landscape, under a sky so immense, I wished I could buy it, fix it up, and live in that landscape.

LEBANON SCHOOL, LEBANON, MISSOURI.
(Right) This austere schoolhouse features an interesting interplay
of double doors and a poled school bell.
(Left) View from the south showing its placement in the town.

(Clockwise from top left)

BRISTER SCHOOL, WINN PARISH, LOUISIANA.
This pretty little structure is unique in having a closed-in front porch to the left of the gable end.

EAST SCHOOL, ALNA, MAINE.
The two doors were most likely used as separate entrances for boys and girls. The upper two windows add a beautiful balancing aesthetic touch to the front end.

TRAPROCK VALLEY SCHOOL, LAKE LINDEN, MICHIGAN.
Built in 1914 in Traprock Valley, it closed in 1940. It was donated to the Houghton County Historical Society in 1979 and moved to its present site in 1983..

WASHINGTON VALLEY SCHOOL, MORRIS TOWNSHIP, NEW JERSEY.
Built in 1869 this finely constructed brick schoolhouse served as a school until 1913. It has been maintained as a treasured community center to this day.

FAIRVIEW SCHOOL, KNOWLTON TOWNSHIP, NEW JERSEY.
Fairview School is a stucco-over-stone construction octagonal school, the only known one to survive in New Jersey. It is interestingly sited within the Fairview cemetery.

NORMAN COUNTY, MINNESOTA.
A tiny school serving farms with large acreage in the western prairie.

WYE OAK SCHOOL, WYE MILLS, MARYLAND.
Wye Oak School represents a gorgeous example of tidewater-brick architecture prevalent in the middle-colony states. It was built sometime in the late 1700s to early 1800s.

The One-Room Schoolhouse **63**

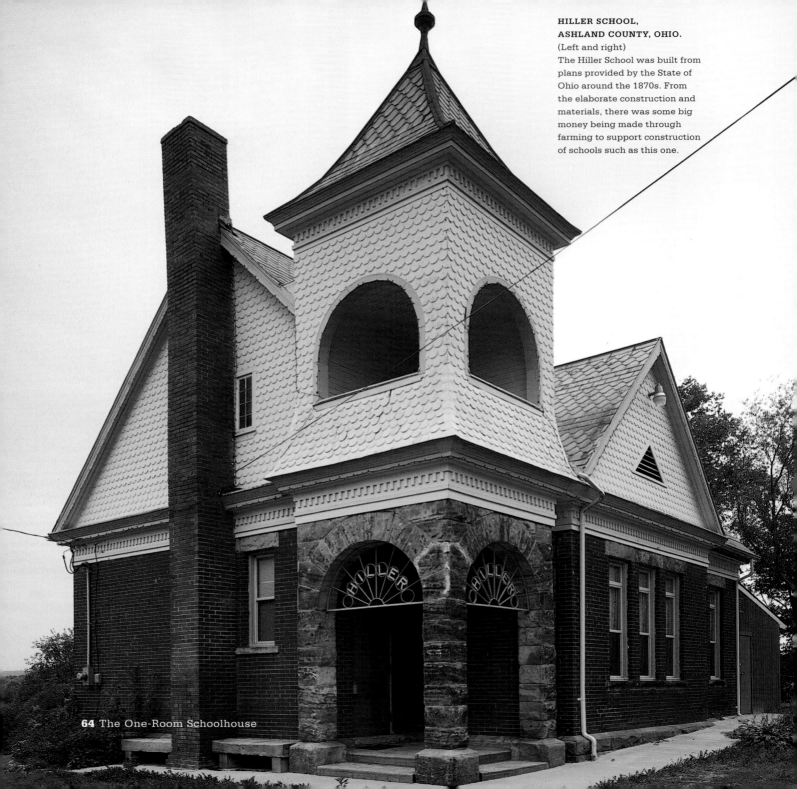

**HILLER SCHOOL,
ASHLAND COUNTY, OHIO.**
(Left and right)
The Hiller School was built from
plans provided by the State of
Ohio around the 1870s. From
the elaborate construction and
materials, there was some big
money being made through
farming to support construction
of schools such as this one.

CROW VALLEY SCHOOL, ORCAS ISLAND, WASHINGTON. (Left)
Set among the tall trees, this school served an island community of
lumberjacks, farmers, and fishermen.

SHADEHILL SCHOOL, SHADEHILL, SOUTH DAKOTA. (Right)
After its closure, this school became a community hall for the small
population remaining in town.

CORRAL SCHOOL, CORRAL, IDAHO.
A fairly large structure, this one-room school might have been partitioned into more rooms when enrollment was large, and may have doubled as a community church for Sunday services. Notice the projected sheds coming out from the building. The left one was for firewood storage, and the one on the right was a barrier to protect the entrance from extreme winds.

HOUGARDY RANCH SCHOOL, ROUNDUP, MONTANA.
Sitting on the second floor of the Musselshell Valley Historical Museum, in the now closed St. Benedict's Catholic School, is the tiny schoolhouse that serviced the Hougardy Ranch and its neighbors.

BERRY COLLEGE, ROME, GEORGIA.
Originally a playhouse for Martha Berry and her siblings, Berry
began using the space in the 1890s to teach local children using her
philosophy of educating the head, hands, and the heart. This was
the birthplace of Berry College.

When her classes became too large, Berry moved them to the then-abandoned Possum Trot Church. Additions made to the left, right, and back became the early college.

PRIVIES.
These "necessaries" came in all types of construction, usually of the same materials as the school they serviced. One important feature they all shared was a very definitive separation between the sexes, sometimes by a fence or wall, but mostly by space—lots of it.

Rita Fox
At her old desk, Gritter Creek School, North English, Iowa.

❝ There was a little neighbor boy named Clarence. Sending a little child to school all by himself was scary, so it was nice to have an older neighbor girl to take him there. If the weather was bad I would walk him all the way back to his house and then return to mine. I always sat next to Clarence, and we became really good friends. He got to really liking me, and when I got married he cried because he had wanted to marry me. ❞

"**I** just love it around here. I've been a lot of places, but these sweet rolling hills—just can't get them out of my blood," said Rita Fox, and I had to agree with her. It was downright beautiful. There is relief on that terrain. And where we were standing, by the Gritter Creek School, you could not see more than a quarter mile away because the top of the hills took away the distance and sent your eyes up into the beautiful blue sky. Rita had been called by the farmer who lived near the school. He had seen me photographing the schoolhouse and came over to say hello. It is very friendly in rural Iowa. After chatting a bit and having me ask questions he could not answer, he asked if I would like to talk to a lady whose passion in life was the preservation of the school and the memorialization of Gritter Creek school stories. Twenty minutes later, Rita was standing to my right as I was taking the last exterior picture. It was only my second day of shooting and recording for this project, and I felt I had hit the motherlode. In her sweet, elderly ladylike way, Rita poured forth stories of her younger days attending school here.

She did not start school here, but close by in the village of North English. Her first year did not fare well, healthwise. She was sick often, and fell behind in learning her first year's work. When her parents bought a farm in the Gritter Creek area, and moved during the second year of schooling for Rita, they were fortunate to have her new teacher, Mimi Rohr, as a close neighbor. As the teacher would head for school from North English in the mornings, she would pick up little Rita in her horse and buggy, "and on the way to and back from school, she taught me my A, B, C's

GRITTER CREEK SCHOOL, NORTH ENGLISH, IOWA.
The interior of the schoolhouse.

and 1, 2, 3's—she took an interest in me." Rita had the chance to return the favor a few years later with a little neighbor boy named Clarence, "Sending a little child to school all by himself was scary, so it was nice to have an older neighbor girl to take him there," says Rita. "If the weather was bad I would walk him all the way back to his house and then return to mine. I always sat next to Clarence, and we became really good friends. He got to really liking me, and when I got married he cried because he had wanted to marry me. He later went to war and was killed."

Helping out in class involved both the voluntary and involuntary participation of students. Voluntarily, older children would take the younger ones under their wings and help them out with their lessons, and when they were up at the front of the room reciting for the teacher, "we were listening anxiously to see how they were progressing with their lessons." Involuntarily, younger students would listen in when the older students were reciting their lessons. "We would listen in on that. It was interesting. We knew what was going on, and we learned that way too, by listening to what we would have to learn in the following years," says Rita.

I was interested in Rita's most vivid memory of school, it was of a new dress. On her first day of school at Gritter Creek, Rita was well turned out for the occasion: "I can close my eyes and still see that plaid dress, it was yellow with brown plaid designs through it. My mother had sent for it from the catalog. It was so pretty and new, and I was so proud of that dress. I was lucky because my parents could afford it, but some girls didn't have as much. We had some very poor people in the area."

Being "poor" was relative among the children of southeast Iowa in the 1920s. One might have more

GRITTER CREEK SCHOOL, NORTH ENGLISH, IOWA.
The brick exterior of the renovated Gritter Creek School. The two privies in the background used to be much further apart.

THE OLD STONE SCHOOL, ROCKFORD, ILLINOIS.
The school's name was carried on from the original stone-built school to this wood-frame replacement. The schoolhouse is now part of Rockford's historic Midway Village.

HUSLEY BEND SCHOOL, INDEPENDENCE COUNTY, ARKANSAS.
West of Newport on a big bend in the White River, sitting on the edge of a farm field, a half mile down a long drive from the highway, is Bill Freeze's gift to all who adore one-room schoolhouses. On his property is Husley Bend School, a school he has lovingly maintained and kept open, for no fee.

than others, though others might have more than you. That situation is reflected in a very poignant story Rita related to me, a story that she says she could only begin to tell when she was much older because of her embarrassment in what she did. However, when she was mature enough to realize that similar experiences happen to all of us, she added it to her repertoire because of its wonderful conclusion. The girls one day were cutting out and coloring paper sun-bonnet girls. "One of the girls in class had a box of crayons with two rows of colors, whereas the rest of us had only one row, and in her box there was a crayon with a new pretty shade of pink. I wanted my sunbonnet girl to be that shade of pink, and I up and stole that color. Well, when it came up missing, the teacher said, 'I am sure it is here somewhere and we will find it before the end of the day.' I didn't know if she knew it was me who took it or not, but at recess I slipped back and put that crayon back into the girl's box. And for years I felt so bad about that, but the teacher had handled it so well, and saved me the embarrassment of being caught with it before I had a chance to return it. Stealing crayons or anything, I was not brought up that way."

I was curious about what they had for lunch in those days. "Almost everyone brought a boiled egg because we didn't have refrigeration, and sometimes we would be treated by our mothers with an orange in our lunch boxes. When we were in the cold weather months, then we could have sandwiches with ground meats. We would keep them in the vestibule along with our coats, with the girls taking the right side and the boys the left side." Much later, at a school-house in Oklahoma, I was shown a room-heating stove with a top that would swivel to allow children to bake potatoes they would bring in for a hot lunch in the wintertime.

One situation unique to one-room schoolhouses, with their collection of all ages, fascinated me, and I received similar responses from most all the women I talked to when I asked about the tattling on siblings for classroom indiscretions. As Rita related, "My little sister was very nice and we were very close, but somehow or other she could not wait to tell mother and dad about what I might have done wrong." It seems that a girl's reaching for perfection sometimes meant standing on the misdeeds of their siblings. But I am sure the brothers or sisters relished the times when they could return the favor.

Rita ended with two privy stories. Before the current school was built, there had been a log school about a hundred yards up the hill. It seems that the school and its outdoor facilities were quite primitive; so primitive, in fact, that the great outdoors sufficed. For privacy there were bushes—two sets of them down the hill from the school, separated by thirty yards. The boys took the closer bushes, and the girls the furthest. Taking into consideration school-age boys' inherent curiosity level about the opposite sex, the arrangement secured more privacy for the girls as they did not have to worry about boys walking by and peeking. When they finally civilized things with the building of a new schoolhouse, complete with state-of-the-art wooden privies, the outhouses were placed in the same general locations. Looking east towards the school, on the left, was the "girls side" privy identified by a star insignia cutout. On the right, a comfortable distance away, was the boy's side privy with the quarter moon insignia. To consolidate space on the property, during restoration of the school, they brought the two structures close together. In all sites that still had the privies in original settings, they were either set well apart, or there was a definite barrier between them.

Rita Fox told me a final tale. The children for about a year became spoiled due to a nice gift from one of the director's wives. "She had been a seamstress at Williamsburg, and had a big box of old cloth patterns that she donated for toilet tissue. Usually we had the hard pages of the three or four Sears & Roebuck or Montgomery Ward catalogs we would go through in a year." And there was an additional benefit, according to Rita: "We girls would sit outside and open those patterns, and we would learn what gussets, darts, pleats, and folds were, and all before we went to high school to take sewing lessons. I loved sewing and I think the reason why was I didn't have to learn a lot of that stuff, I already knew it."

**HUSLEY BEND SCHOOL,
INDEPENDENCE COUNTY, ARKANSAS.**
(Top) There are two entrances to this school. This north entrance has a barrier wall that opens on the east and west sides and acts as a vestibule where children could hang jackets or store muddy rubber boots. It also protected the teacher's back from "surprise intruders."
(Bottom left) Hanging here are three sizes of discipline enforcers.

**HUSLEY BEND SCHOOL,
INDEPENDENCE COUNTY, ARKANSAS.**
Hanging here are various lunch containers used by students.

CANELO SCHOOL, CANELO, ARIZONA.
(Left) The adobe-constructed Canelo School served the local ranches in this beautiful hilly southeast corner of Arizona.
(Right) The rear interior has been preserved as a classroom, while the front of the room is now used for community gatherings.

GRANT SCHOOL, KINGFISHER, OKLAHOMA.
Part of the Chisholm Trail Museum is the Grant School; inside is a lovely stove. It has a top that swings out on which students put their lunches; then the top was swiveled back on so their lunches could be heated.

ROCK HILL SCHOOL, LINN COUNTY, OREGON.
On a hill overlooking the Willamette Valley is the stunning Rock Hill School, so picturesque that it has been filmed repeatedly over the past years. Built in 1910 and used until 1935 when it became a community center, it was purchased in 1960 by Norma and Gilbert Morgan who wanted to preserve its schoolhouse history. It has been lovingly restored by the Rock Hill School Foundation.

**THE ROCK HILL SCHOOL,
LINN COUNTY, OREGON.**
(Left) An elaborate cast iron
school desk with a corn motif
and the words "Patience
Wins" raised in iron.
**THE OLD STONE SCHOOL,
ROCKFORD, ILLINOIS.** (Right)
Now part of Midway Village.
A Sears-Roebuck catalogue
desk.

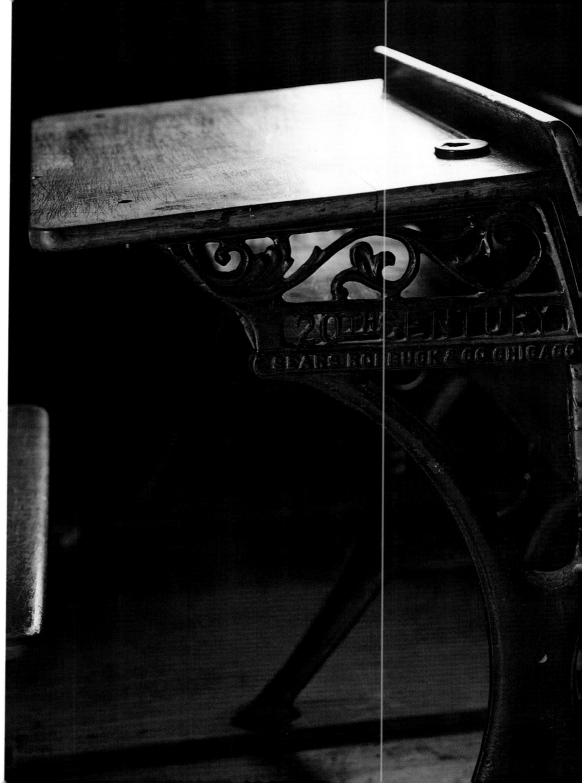

GREEN MOUNTAIN SCHOOL, NEWCASTLE, WYOMING.
On the grounds of Anna Miller Museum is the 1890s Green
Mountain School. It is simple of design, but elegant of line.

(Clockwise from left)

BRENDER CANYON SCHOOL, CASHMERE, WASHINGTON.
Built in the 1830s in Brender Canyon and now part of Pioneer
Village and Museum, this log school was one of the first in the
Cashmere Valley.

GREEN MOUNTAIN SCHOOL, NEWCASTLE, WYOMING.
Interior view of the school.

BRENDER CANYON SCHOOL, CASHMERE, WASHINGTON.
As you look at this interior of the log school, note the white dots
on the upper walls and ceiling. These are natural openings in
the planking that let in cold air during the winter.

BRENDER CANYON SCHOOL, CASHMERE, WASHINGTON.
Ink came in bottles, and in the winter teachers used the warm
ash from the stove to keep it from freezing during the night.

WESTON COUNTY, WYOMING.
An old school, perhaps used as a home for a while, sits in the wide open spaces of eastern Wyoming, reflecting a time when the landscape was less open, with more farms and ranches, and lots of kids to fill up that big space.

**MISSION RIDGE SCHOOLHOUSE,
POINT PLEASANT, WEST VIRGINIA.**
(Left) In the collection of buildings at the West Virginia State
Farm Museum is Mission Ridge Schoolhouse. A very plain exterior
does not prepare one for the brightly painted interior that lifts
one's spirits upon entering the building.
(Right) Old photos of the former students humanize the space.

COBBLESTONE SCHOOL, CHILDS, NEW YORK. (Left)
Now part of the Cobblestone Society Museum, this 1849
building is unique in that it is a wooden structure with only
a cobblestone veneer.
OLD LOG SCHOOLHOUSE, MOUNTAIN VIEW, ARKANSAS. (Right)
Originally built as a homestead, the Old Log Schoolhouse of
the Ozark Folk Center was converted to school use in the 1920s
and 1930s. It was used for only during the summer months
when the children were not needed for farm duties.

**LANESDALE SCHOOL,
BALSAM LAKE, WISCONSIN.**
Saved and restored by the
Polk County Historical Society,
Lanesdale School has one of
the better appointed interiors
I had seen.

LANESDALE SCHOOL
1874—1962
SEC. 29 — LAKETOWN TWP.

115

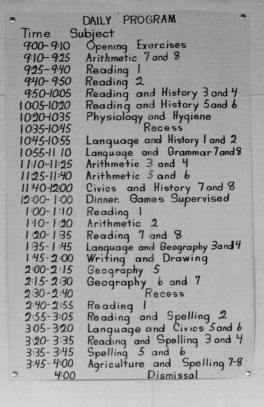

DAILY PROGRAM

Time	Subject
9:00 – 9:10	Opening Exercises
9:10 – 9:25	Arithmetic 7 and 8
9:25 – 9:40	Reading 1
9:40 – 9:50	Reading 2
9:50 – 10:05	Reading and History 3 and 4
10:05 – 10:20	Reading and History 5 and 6
10:20 – 10:35	Physiology and Hygiene
10:35 – 10:45	Recess
10:45 – 10:55	Language and History 1 and 2
10:55 – 11:10	Language and Grammar 7 and 8
11:10 – 11:25	Arithmetic 3 and 4
11:25 – 11:40	Arithmetic 5 and 6
11:40 – 12:00	Civics and History 7 and 8
12:00 – 1:00	Dinner. Games Supervised
1:00 – 1:10	Reading 1
1:10 – 1:20	Arithmetic 2
1:20 – 1:35	Reading 7 and 8
1:35 – 1:45	Language and Geography 3 and 4
1:45 – 2:00	Writing and Drawing
2:00 – 2:15	Geography 5
2:15 – 2:30	Geography 6 and 7
2:30 – 2:40	Recess
2:40 – 2:55	Reading 1
2:55 – 3:05	Reading and Spelling 2
3:05 – 3:20	Language and Civics 5 and 6
3:20 – 3:35	Reading and Spelling 3 and 4
3:35 – 3:45	Spelling 5 and 6
3:45 – 4:00	Agriculture and Spelling 7-8
4:00	Dismissal

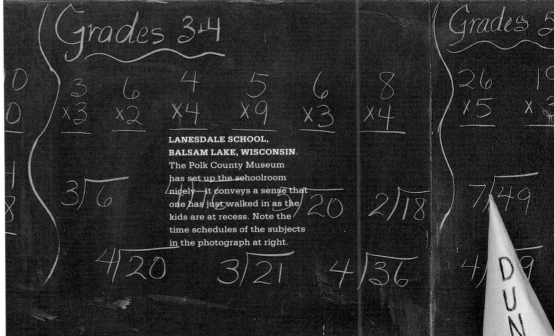

LANESDALE SCHOOL, BALSAM LAKE, WISCONSIN.
The Polk County Museum has set up the schoolroom nicely—it conveys a sense that one has just walked in as the kids are at recess. Note the time schedules of the subjects in the photograph at right.

GAINEVILLE SCHOOL, GAINEVILLE, UTAH.
This simple wooden structure served the purposes of school, town hall, community center, and voting hall. What makes it special is its incredibly beautiful setting of the Fremont River Valley and the South Gaineville Mesa and Blue Hills, adjacent to Highway 24 on the way to Capitol Reef National Park.

TORREY LOG SCHOOL AND CHURCH, TORREY, UTAH. Torrey Log School and Church was built in 1898 by Mormon settlers who furnished the labor and materials for this unique log structure with a hip roof, flared eaves, square bell tower, and pink-sandstone foundation.

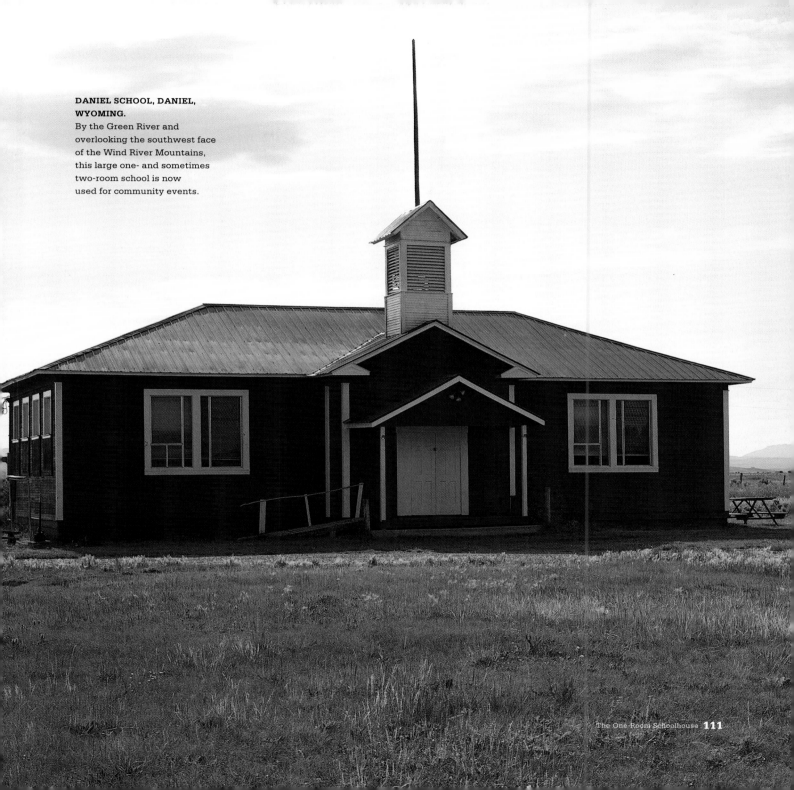

DANIEL SCHOOL, DANIEL, WYOMING.
By the Green River and overlooking the southwest face of the Wind River Mountains, this large one- and sometimes two-room school is now used for community events.

**THE STONE SCHOOL AND TAYLOR SCHOOL,
KANKAKEE, ILLINOIS.**
A contrast of two time periods and materials in school construction:
the stone school dates to 1869 and the wooden-frame school to
1904. Both are on the grounds of the Kankakee Historical Society.

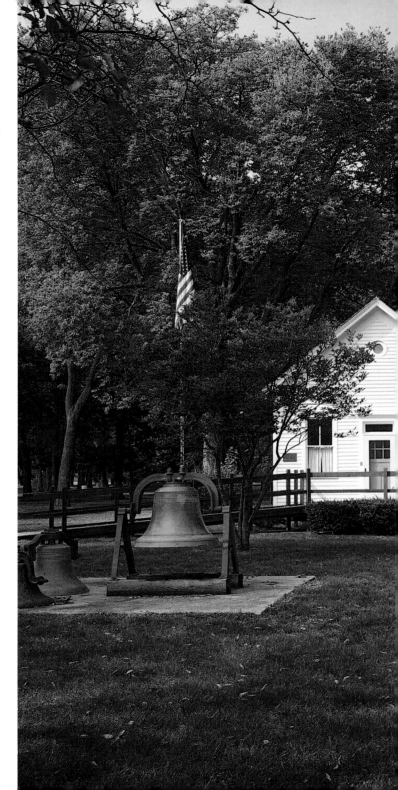

ROUND SCHOOL, BROOKLINE, VERMONT.
Built in 1822 by Dr. John Wilson, this is the only known round brick schoolhouse to have been built in the United States; it served as a school until 1929. To minimize the discomforts of New England winters, a wood shed with a privy built into its left end was attached to the school.

**NORTHEAST SCHOOLHOUSE, DISTRICT #1,
RICHMOND, MASSACHUSETTS.**
This schoolhouse, photographed in an old-fashioned New England
snowstorm, was the impetus for this book.

Mrs. Avis Kautzmann
Retired teacher of the Mandan school system, and one time
teacher at Sweet Briar School, Mandan, North Dakota.

"Us retired teachers, we'll be up there at the Capitol, don't worry about us. For those of us that have taught in a rural school, we don't want those schools changed. We don't want to have the children riding the school buses an hour and a half in the morning and an hour and a half in the afternoon; it is ridiculous. Eventually it will probably happen, but as long as some us older ones are there, going to the Capitol and testifying, it might give them a few more years."

Originally, I had planned to introduce Mrs. Avis Kautzmann in the sixth chapter, where I profile the Sweet Briar School; Mrs. Kautzmann had taught there for a year. However, in exploring the three most nostalgic parts of the one-room schoolhouse experience—the structures, the students and their perspective, and finally from the teachers' point of view—I could not hold back on having Mrs. Kautzmann speak here on behalf of the ideal teacher. Not only was she educated in a one-room school, but had taught in several. Later, she moved to a city school district and spent the remainder of her teaching career in a normal consolidated system of individual grades. She was privy to an insider's savvy perspective on the differences and benefits of one system over another. And she was not afraid to express a frank opinion.

Mrs. Kautzmann (in my respect for elderly teachers, I am not comfortable using first names) after college began teaching at the Golden Valley rural school. She transferred to Sweet Briar rural school in 1942 to live with her father who had a house in the town of the same name. It was the beginning of the war and her husband had gone into the Air Force and was stationed in Florida. The school was just a short walk north from the tiny community of about twenty buildings. The town hugged the tracks of Burlington Northern Railroad. Mrs. Kautzmann did not feel isolated out there, not with four passenger trains stopping each day on their way to and from Bismarck. Today if you go down by the tracks there is not much left. The farms have gotten larger so there are fewer people. With cars, obtaining the necessities of living and farming is but a twenty-minute trip to Mandan. It was a different world back then, and I asked Mrs. Kautzmann what it was like to teach at the school.

CRABAPPLE SCHOOL, CRABAPPLE, TEXAS.
In some states it was tough to secure land to build schools on, but in this Germanic community it was an honor to donate the land. Settler Machias Schmidt, by winning a foot race, won that honor, and in 1878 the limestone Crabapple School was built.

CRABAPPLE SCHOOL, CRABAPPLE, TEXAS. Visible from the back of Crabapple School are horse stalls, and further to the left, a home for the resident teacher, called a teacherage.

"Heavenly," she replied. "The pupils came to learn, and there were hardly any discipline problems. Parents expected them to learn, and saw to it they had their homework done. If there was a discipline problem, you told the parents and they took care of it. It was heaven, especially compared to my last couple of years of teaching."

Mrs. Kautzmann compared rural schools to the urban: "In the rural setting, the older students would serve as mentors for the younger ones and help them if the teacher was busy with another group of children. They would also help with the work, because when you had a rural school, first thing you had to be your own janitor. And you had to keep the fires going, clean out the ashes, and things like that—it kept the children busy. I had about sixteen pupils and no teacher's aide. I had a coal stove and kerosene lights, no electricity back then. It was a new school built by the WPA, it was warm and comfortable."

There were 180 days in the school session, and every one of those days had to be accounted for. This was a rural area, however, and the farms needed their boys to be available at the crucial time of planting and harvesting, so some creative scheduling took place to accommodate the necessities of farm life. It was the war years in 1942, and some of the older sons had been inducted or enlisted in the service, leaving a shortage of help in the fields. One of the parents, representing several families, approached Mrs. Kautzmann with a proposal for providing more time for the planting season in spring. "It is not up to me," she said, "but if you are asking me if I will teach on a Saturday, yes, and I will cut the Christmas vacation short, as long as you get the permission of the school board and the district supervisor. I was okay with that because I wanted to go to Miami where my husband was stationed in the Army Air Force, and the sooner the better. The kids got out around the end of April or the beginning of May, and some of the older kids were home and available to help with putting the crop in and other chores during that busy season."

I asked her to contrast her fourth-grade class in the town of Mandan to that of the rural Sweet Briar. "Cooperation of the parents," Mrs. Kautzmann replied. "In the rural setting, it seems the parents are all out there for the children. When we had teacher-parent conferences in Mandan, we had problems getting some parents in. The [parents of] students that were doing well were there. Those that weren't, were not there. Then there were the one-parent families, and nobody came. We had a difficult time getting either of the two [parents] to come. And when I could get them both in, it was nothing but a fight between the [parents]. I got to say very little. I am now part of the RIF [Reading Is Fundamental] program, and we go out to Sweet Briar a couple of times a year and distribute books. We are so welcome out there. I was a remedial reading teacher here in Mandan. The children didn't care to take a book home, and if they did I don't think they read it. If it was read, it was by a parent or sibling."

Remaining one-room public schools in this country are tenuously holding on to a tradition that school officials and legislators want to eliminate. Sweet Briar is no exception. They have pleaded their case to the legislators to keep the school open and so far have been successful. However, it is not easy, but they do have Mrs. Kautzmann on their side. As she said, "Us retired teachers, we'll be up there at the Capitol, don't worry about us. For those of us that have taught in a rural school, we don't want those schools changed. We don't want to have the children riding the school buses an hour and a half in the morning and an hour and a half in the afternoon; it is ridiculous. Eventually it will probably happen, but as long as some us older ones are there, going to the Capitol and testifying, it might give them a few more years."

I was sad to learn that Mrs. Kautzmann passed away two months after our interview, but I cannot help thinking that spiritually she is still using her pull and tenacity to fight the good fight for the upkeep of traditional rural education.

ELGIN SCHOOL, ELGIN, NEVADA.
Most of Nevada is remote; the little town of Elgin, in an incredibly beautiful narrow valley, fits the pattern. Still, the small population managed to save and restore this handsome school as both a community center and as a historical school.

ELGIN SCHOOL, ELGIN, NEVADA.
The teacherage was a planned attachment to the back of the school. In this view of the kitchen, notice the hallway separating the living quarters from the classroom. The bedroom was through the door on the left.

Chapter Four

"The Good Fight": Preservation and Restoration

CADENTOWN SCHOOL, CADENTOWN, KENTUCKY. A Rosenwald school awaiting funds for renovation.

It was twenty-three years ago when I first visited Lexington, Kentucky. I was scheduled to photograph another book, Shaker Furniture, some thirty miles west of Lexington at Pleasant Hill Shaker Village. Running early, I toured the city and the surrounding farms. With a good map, I made my way around the city on loop roads that brought sights of the most beautiful horse farms in America: acres and acres of black- or white-fenced horse pastures, with some of the finest examples of American thoroughbreds as one could find. I fell in love with Lexington. In the intervening years, every trip close to the city gave the opportunity for glimpsing again some of the views I had seen on that first trip.

I had felt a growing sadness with each subsequent trip to the city, though, as farms and open spaces were becoming casualties of suburban sprawl. Granted, the population was growing and people needed housing, but if I had one major fault to find with the new developments in Lexington (and most suburbs in general), it's that little or no space was allotted for parks or other public space for residents to enjoy as a community. Where good developers had used intelligence, foresight, and a little humanity, the consequences were financially rewarding for both the developer and the residents. Not only was the quality of life better, but even more important (especially to the people who live by the bottom line), the value of their property showed higher appreciation than that of developments that packed them in as tight as possible. Unfortunately, most developers haven't been so kind, leading to the dehumanizing sprawl we are so used to today. So, I became quite intrigued when I learned from Bill MacIntire of the Kentucky Heritage Council about a woman named Jonetta Young, who was taking on developers in the process of saving a very important part of local black educational history, the Cadentown School. I made arrangements to meet her and to see the school.

Jonetta Young, on the young side of middle age, is a black woman with some Native American ancestry. I found her to be a gutsy, determined, proud, humorous, and generally personable lady. She was in the trenches doing the dirty work of preservation, taking on the abuse generated by vested interests, fighting the good fight as a grunt (a very sympathetic and respected word for some of us) along with a few other dependable neighbors. They had stopped a planned development that would have taken down the school and the community's abandoned black church and that would have isolated or destroyed a historic black cemetery, and would have generally removed most traces of a once flourishing black village called Cadentown. Cadentown dated from just after the Civil War, when the newly freed slaves were given the right to purchase land and build modest homes.

At its peak Cadentown had about 200 black inhabitants but was now represented by only about twenty-five, of which Jonetta was a relatively recent addition. It was after Jonetta was in a severe car accident and recuperating at her mother's home in Cadentown that she became part of the neighborhood. While recovering, she began taking walks in the neighborhood looking at the old school, the church, and important spaces like the community well where the early residents once fetched their water. All those walks brought back the stories her mother had told about growing up in a close and warm neighborhood. "My mother said, 'the kids would gather by the well during recess in the hot

CADENTOWN SCHOOL, CADENTOWN, KENTUCKY.
Jonetta Young, in front of the Rosenwald school she is trying to preserve.

HILDRED SCHOOL, NICHOLAS COUNTY, KENTUCKY.
(Top left) The Hildred School in its isolated setting.
(Bottom left) To prevent vandalism and theft, the interior has been stripped of all furnishings.
(Right) The blackboard calendar from May 1941 that has remained unscathed all these years.

days of the school year and have water fights, the girls against the boys.' Just the way she was describing those times, I wish I could have been around in those days—except with the modern conveniences. I wouldn't be for packing water. Bessie Westley, a neighbor of ours, told me that in those days you went to school to learn, not to goof off. All the teacher had to do was tell your parents that their child had been bad, and it was bad times for you. Even before you got home the whole community would get on you, 'I heard you was bad—swat.' And you'd think, Oh my, when I get home I'm going to get swatted again. Mother would tell of the teachers she had, some very strict, but one she especially liked, Lena May Howard, is still lively and looking great for all her years. We went to visit her recently and she recognized my mother immediately, and started telling her how good of a student she was and how she liked having her in class. My mother floated home."

Jonetta has made much progress in preserving the important characteristics of the community. With help with a grant from the state heritage council, the Cadentown School is to be restored, and a small park will protect the important historical treasures. On the north side of the property an abandoned rail line will soon be turned into a community walking, skating, and bike trail by the Rails for Trails Parks Fund. As bright a prospect as this sounds, prevailing economic conditions were making the allotted funds hard to come by. Also, a developer whom she and her preservation friends had defeated a few years back has resurfaced, in cahoots with a local church in trying to grab as much open land as they can for an expansion of their facilities. The preservationists' fight continues to try stopping irreversible damage.

Before I left, I asked Jonetta about the response from the community to what had been accomplished so far. "Fine," she said. "They were appreciative of what we had achieved." "And your mother?" I inquired. In a wispy voice, Jonetta told me the words her mother used to express her gratitude, "I am so happy that someone cared about preserving this area. I am so proud of you."

Gladys Shrout has the bearing of a lady of sophistication, sporting a very trim and attractive look, dressed in slacks and an exquisite silk blouse, very fine threads for where we were going to end up. I had met her in the town of Carlisle, where she was working at the Nicholas County tourism office. We were probably no more than thirty-five miles away from Jonetta's project in Lexington, and it was fascinating to compare not just the differences but also the even greater similarities of both projects and the women behind them. Where Jonetta was pretty laidback, Gladys was high-keyed. It was also clear that Gladys was part of the area's society that made things happen. At dinner parties she would be able to grab the ear of guests and expound on the virtues of saving and protecting local treasures. Her infectious enthusiasm probably made many converts over the years. She was not shy in wielding her position in the community to make good things happen, and as she said to me, "preservation is my passion." The two women might have come from different social strata, but both were passionate about preserving what they thought was something of great importance to the local community, and they were going to fight for what they believed in whatever way worked for them.

Gladys was very cordial and wanted to help me, but she also was anxious to proceed with the story of the Hildred schoolhouse, which she was in the process of saving. We jumped into our vehicles and proceeded

to the town's consolidated school grounds and the site of where the one-room schoolhouse was to be placed after its removal from its original site. Besides saving the little school because it was a treasure, the school system was going to use it to show the children of the community how their education would have differed in a one-room school in earlier days. This was an objective of many saved one-roomers that I had come across in my travels—giving today's young students a glimpse back in time.

Another reason for moving the school: it was in such a remote area that it would have been hard to reach and to protect from vandalism. I could understand the remoteness issue. After leaving the town school grounds we drove about ten miles east of town before we pulled off of the highway and turned onto a narrow two-lane country road. We were on that but a short distance before turning onto a one-lane road for another mile or so. With her full-sized sedan and my big old Ford van, we were most fortunate not to have met anyone coming the opposite way. To get to the school we turned onto a dirt path that climbed up a short knoll through a small patch of woods and into a clearing where the school had been sited when built in the late 1790s.

Gladys told me of how the school had been bought by a Louise Limbal for $65.00 from the school district some time after it had closed in 1941 because of her love for it. With time her son A. K. Limbal took over ownership, and it was through him that Gladys was eventually going to get the school donated to the county. A. K. Limbal required a bit of coaxing, with a

DISTRICT #5 SCHOOL, ABOLITE, INDIANA.
The renovated District #5 School now serves Allen County (greater Fort Wayne) as a site of historical scholastic significance.

DISTRICT #5 SCHOOL, ABOLITE, INDIANA.
(Left) Interior period setting used as an example for
showing today's pupils what their great-grandparents
might have experienced.
(Top right) View to entrance vestibule.
(Bottom right) An actual blackboard—a wooden board
painted black—it was used before slate became the
fashion.

DISTRICT #3 SCHOOL, LAFAYETTE, INDIANA. (Left) Interior of the Bartling residence showing main schoolroom, which is now used as a living room. (Right) Entrance vestibule showing original side cloak rooms.

One-Room Schoolhouse

little help of his daughter, who had a doctorate in education, to finally give his approval. He had been reluctant to have the school moved, feeling that it had sat in its spot for so long that that was where it belonged, but with time he came around to see Gladys's point—that to leave it at the site was to jeopardize its existence. He was not to live long enough to sign the papers, unfortunately, but his wife followed his wishes, and the school was signed over to the Carlisle tourism bureau and the Nicholas County Historical Society in the spring of 2002. The cost of moving it was going to be high and the two organizations were to share some of the expenses, once Gladys had worked her way through her sources of volunteer labor, that is.

Leave a building alone for a short period of time and nature's critters quickly become squatters in the space. As Gladys opened the school's door we could see the activities of squirrels, mice, bees, spiders, opossums, and all other types of interlopers. Gladys was not fazed nor did she seem concerned about her nice clothes (this was a definite dungaree situation), but just pushed in and showed me about. She told me how in the l980s the building had been used to film a television production of Huckleberry Finn, and part of the deal with the producers was that they were to paint the exterior of the building white after shooting was completed. The building before that was a weathered gray clapboard, unpainted like most schools were in their earlier years. Paint was expensive and very labor-intensive to make prior to its commercial production, which began the latter part of the nineteenth century.

We went to the blackboard where a most haunting piece of ephemeral history still existed. With white and colored chalk the month of May was written on the slate board from the year the school closed in 1941. How that had managed to remain all these years with-out being obliterated was beyond my and Gladys's comprehension. I mentioned to her how wonderful it was that this was going to be properly protected and how she must reflect on her efforts at times. She replied, "I love history. I feel I'm a very good historian. I'm going to love to see this school restored because I love renovation. It is my passion."

I was led to interesting one-room schoolhouses in a variety of ways: by recommendation, by listings in books and on the Internet, and sometimes by blind luck. Reverend Linn Bartling's beautifully renovated brick schoolhouse fell into that last category. I was looking for a school in Aboite, Indiana, that I had heard about from the state historical office. Without specific directions, I followed a route that indicated the very small town of Aboite just south of the U.S. highway I was traveling on. Not knowing it at the time I was going in the opposite direction of where I should have been going, but because of that mistake I went by T.P. District #3 school. Momentarily thinking I had found what I was looking for, I stopped. As I proceeded to the door and knocked, I had the suspicion that I had made a mistake because it looked like a residence. Reverend Bartling, who just happened to be home preparing her Sunday sermon, greeted me warmly, especially when I explained how I had gotten to her door.

Her building was very similar to the one I was looking for. She told me that I had gone the wrong way, but asked if I would like to see how she and her husband had converted their school into a living space. Ever the voyeur, I took up her hospitality with enthusiasm. Once inside, I realized what a discerning job they had done with the structure, and when I went to the school I originally was looking for, I found that

JICARILLA SCHOOL, LINCOLN COUNTY, NEW MEXICO. The Jicarilla School is now being fought over by the few remaining locals who want to preserve it and by the National Forest Service that wants to tear it down.

SUMMIT HILL SCHOOL, CHANUTE, KANSAS. (Left)
Patsy Smeed's converted schoolhouse living room shows
on the left the original plastering over stone finish. The exposed
stone work was an aesthetic decision, and not original to the
space when it was used as a school.

STRICKLAND SCHOOL, LEON COUNTY, FLORIDA. (Above)
On the property of Elvy Carter, Strickland School, built in
the 1870s, awaits the time when, with a little extra time and
cash, Mr. Carter can properly renovate the building.

The One-Room Schoolhouse **143**

they had kept the integrity of the school intact. To convert it into a home, the Bartlings had only made two major changes: they made a second-floor bedroom in the main schoolroom and attached an addition to the rear, faced with brick to blend with the rest of the building. It looked so good that I asked and received permission to take a few photographs.

While photographing, Linn told me the story of how they came to purchase and renovate the building. Linn's husband had taken a job on the west side of Fort Wayne, and to make the commute to work easier they started to look for a piece of property on that side of town to fix up (they loved to renovate old structures). They were looking for an old brick farmhouse, but found none available at that moment. In the paper they saw the schoolhouse up for auction, went to look at it, fell in love, and became the high bidder after a spirited bout with the developer of a high-end development right next door to the school (a complex that, surprisingly, looks pretty good). Later the developer said that if he had known at that time what they were going to do with the property he would not have bid so high to protect his investment. From pictures Linn showed me, it was clear that the structure was not in great shape when they purchased it. They enlisted help from friends to strip the interior so they could insulate the walls properly, and they hired a contractor with whom they had a good relationship from a previous renovation. He converted the attic into a second-floor bedroom, made the rear addition, and both fixed the old brickwork and faced the new addition with similar brick. If you have ever owned an old home, you will know what an effort it is to perform work like this. Spare time is nonexistent while in the midst of such a project. Frustration with the time required, or with the swelling mound of invoices from the contractor, sometimes leads to shortcuts. From what I saw and heard, the Bartlings had known from previous experiences what they were getting into and completed it as they wanted to and not too far over budget. They were rewarded with a stunning home, and quite a fitting tribute to Linn, who had spent most of her life in education.

Linn knew the schoolhouse I had originally been looking for, and was acquainted with the lady who could let me in to see it. With a lucky phone call to her house—she had been home for a few minutes to walk her dog—we made arrangements to meet and to see Aboite T.P. District #5 school. What a beautiful structure, almost a twin of the Bartlings' renovated school. In both these structures, the way the interiors were laid out, the style of architecture, and the construction materials were all dictated by the state. In the 1880s Ohio and Indiana were quite prosperous from farming very rich soil and from having great markets available for their harvest because of the railroad and the canal linkages to the large East Coast cities. Many of these states' residents had migrated from the Northeast where education had always been important, and where there was a very liberal strain of thought that emphasized public education. Looking at the images of this school, one can see the pride of the community back then and what the citizens wanted for their children. Their desire was expressed in the amount of money they put into the public education system. That pride was carried on to the present day, because they did a marvelous job in saving this structure and having it placed on school grounds so today's children could learn about a previous century's school life. This was what the Hildred School in Carlisle, Kentucky, was going to be like when those folks finished moving and restoring their building.

MCCRAY SCHOOL, ALAMANCE COUNTY, NORTH CAROLINA.
This tiny, simple framed building dates to the early twentieth century and was a school for rural African-American children.

atsy Smeeds's limestone schoolhouse in Chanute, Kansas, has hints of Mike Rakosnik's schoolhouse in Nebraska (mentioned in the third chapter). The school had been adjacent to Patsy's family's farm from the beginning, and more than three generations received their education within its four walls. As with Mike Rakosnik, when the school closed, the family found it in their best interest to purchase the structure from the school district. Patsy's brother was interested in converting it to a residence, but his efforts stalled through lack of money or enthusiasm. Patsy's husband at the time was teaching art at a college in Pittsburgh, Kansas, a town within commuting distance of the schoolhouse. They bought it from her brother and started the backbreaking task of renovating it by themselves, with some crucial help from Patsy's father. Patsy said her father was "unbelievable in his willingness to provide labor, machinery, and building expertise [he was a farmer, and farmers have to know a lot to be able to survive]. Without him we may never have gotten through this."

They found dilapidated barns with some sound timber that they were given permission to cart off free of charge. They also were able to do the same with the stones they needed. It was a scrounge job of the first order, but carried off with a great sense of style since both were artists—and, as Patsy said to me, "kind of hippies during that time period." Though the project took some time to complete, when it was finished, they had one of the more unusual structures in the state of Kansas. To this they added an original claim shack (the kind of building you had to build to be eligible for a homesteading deed of land). It was moved from a mile away, again with her father's help, as the need for extra space became necessary, and of course done with their indelible sense of style.

MCCRAY SCHOOL, ALAMANCE COUNTY, NORTH CAROLINA.
The interior of the McCray school, restored to its earlier glory, is used by the county school system to depict life in a one-room schoolhouse in the 1900s.

BELLVIEW SCHOOL, CARTHAGE, NORTH CAROLINA.
(Below) Bellview School is on the grounds of the Moore County School Board. Classic in style, it dates to the early twentieth century.
(Right) This view is from the open vestibule of the Bellview School looking into the front of the classroom.

Chapter Five

Special Schools, Special Histories

PHILLIPS SCHOOL, ATLANTA, LOUISIANA. Restored and loved by the local small black community, Phillips School has had a proud history of educating many outstanding citizens in this area of the state.

As discussed in the first two chapters, religion influenced U.S. education significantly during the early part of the Colonial Era, slightly less during the latter Colonial and early Federalist period, and only marginally as public schools became dominant during and after the Civil War. As religion lost its primary grasp on the nation's educational systems, it continued in a strong secondary position, providing a faith-based alternative to an increasingly secular nation. Scrutinizing proposed state and federal laws for any threats to sectarian influence, the various religious denominations, sometimes acting in concert, would flex their political muscles to maintain a presence in the U.S. educational community.

Catholicism was one of the strongest groups to influence religious education in this country. Catholic schools spread rapidly, especially in urban areas where the most immigrants, many of whom were Catholic, settled—and they also opened their doors to the non-Catholic poor. Although their classes rarely took place in one-room schoolhouses, since their students came from areas of high population density, Catholic school systems made an important contribution by influencing U.S. laws, keeping them benevolent to the ideas of religious education. This, in turn, supported the efforts of smaller sects to adhere to a total lifestyle based on their religious convictions and to provide faith-based education, often in small schools around the country.

For instance, the Germanic religious sects, such as the Amish, the Hutterites, and the conservative wing of the Mennonites flourished in an atmosphere created by sympathetic laws that accepted their pacifism and their desire to educate their children according to the tenets of their religion.

The Amish and the Hutterites, with their rural agricultural society and their desire to forsake modern transportation, have contributed to a continuing use of small, conveniently placed schoolhouses. They treasure the simplicity of having a school that is only an easy walk or a buggy ride away. These schools follow an old tradition of extending only to the eighth grade, which is believed by the community to be sufficient school education for their rural agricultural lifestyles and conservative religious beliefs. The Amish, in particular, continue to grow, expanding from their original settlements in eastern Pennsylvania to the Midwest and on into the high plains. They, in their ever-expanding communities, have kept alive the tradition of the one-room schoolhouse.

The Shakers, a religious group from the past now represented almost completely by village museums, also had a strong impact on one-room education. Originally associated with the Quaker religion in England, a small group of "Shaking Quakers" (so called because of their fervent dancing and singing during services) immigrated to America in 1776. They founded a colony in the Albany, New York, area and actively sought converts to their beliefs of celibacy, pacifism, and separation from the world. By the 1840s their numbers had grown to 4,000, living in twenty-five villages, eighteen of which were fairly large and long-lasting. Since they were a celibate sect, the group's growth came from converts— often entire families— and from foster children, whom they cared for and educated in return for the children's community labor. All the Shaker villages had small schools run by the brothers and sisters of the commu-

PHILLIPS SCHOOL, ATLANTA, LOUISIANA.
Alumni of the Phillips School, clockwise from top left: Grace Clay, Shirley Drewitt, Betty Washington, and Alex Sapp.

nity. Later, when their religious fervor had mellowed, neighboring children from "the world outside" were allowed to attend their schools, so the Shakers were able to instill in many children some of the work and life philosophy that characterized them, even though the sect eventually died out.

As early as the Colonial Era, some religious groups, particularly the Quakers, spoke of society's responsibility to school Native Americans and African-born slaves who were being brought into the country. Part of their motive grew from the missionaries' zeal to convert them to Christianity, and their progressive belief that these populations should be given the ability to read and to understand the teachings of the Bible, just like the European-based population. While African-Americans lived within white America, Native Americans were often moved to reservations in remote areas, separated from mainstream America. Further, their children were often forcibly sent to boarding schools far away from family and friends, where teachers unsympathetic to their cultural ways and heritage taught them. Lessons were taught in English, a language foreign to them, and school books—standard texts used throughout the country—referenced little-known cultural aspects of white society.

Four African-American schools.
(Clockwise from top left)
IRON HILL SCHOOL, NEW CASTLE, DELAWARE.
The Iron Hill School was funded by Pierre S. Dupont.
BYNUM ROSENWALD SCHOOL, PANOLA COUNTY, MISSISSIPPI.
LINCOLN BRICK SCHOOL, CANTON, MISSOURI.
The Lincoln Brick School is currently in a fight for restoration.
"THE LITTLE WHITE SCHOOLHOUSE,"
CHOCCOLOCCO, ALABAMA.
Choccolocco's school for black children is now used as a community center.

Missionary schools also engaged in this approach to "education." When I photographed the Bear Mountain Episcopal Indian Mission School in Amherst County, Virginia, I happened upon the school the afternoon just before a big pow-wow and rededication ceremony following a major renovation. Coming to the celebration was a Native American gentleman and his wife who stopped to talk to me as I set up my large camera to record the school. In talking with him, I found out that his mother had attended the school. Excited, I asked if I could interview him for the stories she had told him of her youth going to the school, but his reaction, though friendly, was curious. Stepping back from me, slightly, he said, "My mother never spoke of those days." He let it go at that; I got the message.

Dwight Mission School near Marble City, Oklahoma, on the very eastern side of the state, is another missionary school of note. This school was on the reservation where the Cherokee were forced to relocate to during the Trail of Tears walk, when they were driven out of their homelands during the administration of Andrew Jackson. Of all the tribes, the Cherokee had been the most adaptable to the white man's ways, farming, raising cattle, developing a written language, and forming a constitution. Forced relocation tore through their heart like a lance. At the end of their trail was the Dwight Mission School, originally founded in 1818 in Arkansas and moved to the present site in Oklahoma in 1829. Founded by Reverend Chephas Washburn from New England, it served the Cherokee community as a coeducational school. As an information plaque on the small building explained, "Reverend Washburn forsook an aristocratic life to come to the frontier to live among a people who had been banished from their home, and whose language he did not understand. He suffered diseases, privations, and inadequate financial support as well as the indifference of the Indian families." These two sentences probably reflect the good and the bad as poignantly as anything else that can be said—good deeds being done with a Presbyterian slant for a people who had rightfully come to distrust the whole of white society.

African-American culture shared with Native Americans the ugliness of discrimination and persecution by the dominant white population. Not being isolated geographically like the Native Americans, African-American daily life in slaveless states followed an existence similar to the white community's. However, blacks lived in neighborhoods where the schools were all-black. A result of the 1896 case Plessy v. Ferguson, in which the Supreme Court declared "separate but equal" laws constitutional, segregation set the tone for black education, especially in the South. It remained so until the 1960s, when the landmark Supreme Court ruling Brown v. Board of Education found "separate but equal" inherently unequal. It should be noted, though, that even during segregation, integrated schools did exist in some districts, particularly in the North. And, in more rural school districts, due to smaller populations, the integration of black pupils with whites often occurred in the towns' one-room schoolhouses.

Under slavery, black education consisted primarily of vocational training geared toward running a plantation. In rare situations a sympathetic slave-

OLD ARKANA SCHOOL, BAXTER COUNTY, ARKANSAS.
Old Arkana School is a two-roomer, but when I walked to the back, there was a seam going down the middle that indicated it probably started as one room and then grew as extra space was needed.

owning family might have taught an interested slave how to read and write. After the Civil War, when slaves were granted freedom, they grouped together in small villages, and as in small white towns, they had little one-room schoolhouses. Money to pay for teachers, supplies, and the maintenance of large buildings was scarce throughout the South generally; for the black schools, it was even worse. The famous African-American educator Booker T. Washington once declared, "Many of the places in the South where the schools are taught are as bad as stables."

It was in meeting Booker T. Washington and getting a firsthand account of the deplorable conditions of black education that Julius Rosenwald, president of Sears & Roebuck, awarded him $25,000 dollars in 1912 for his Tuskegee Institute and to build six new schools in economically depressed Alabama. The success of those schools inspired Rosenwald, one of the country's biggest benefactors to black education, to continue the program until his death in 1936. Using a challenge-grant approach, the Rosenwald school fund would match monies pledged by the local African Americans and sympathetic whites and then count on the remainder of the money to come from the public treasury. In twenty-two years Rosenwald gave close to $4.5 million, which was the stimulus to build just under 5,000 schools. Efforts today are underway to save the Rosenwald schools as an historical testament to black education in the South.

Another philanthropist who made an impact on black education was Delaware industrialist Pierre Dupont. A new school code passed in Delaware in the early 1900s made no provisions for supporting "separate but equal" black school systems. Dupont took it upon himself, in the spirit of educational philanthropy, to renovate or build all eighty-nine African-American schools in the state of Delaware, in a project that came to be known as "the Delaware experiment." A story in Time magazine commented, "While some men choose to make money, Dupont chooses to make citizens."

It was in one of those Dupont structures, the Iron Hill School built in 1929, that I had the fortunate chance to meet and talk with Laura Mackie Lee. The school is now a museum of natural history, and Laura is the museum director. She has taken a keen interest in the history of the school, and has become quite the expert. Her explanation for Dupont's aid to black education was, "It seemed to be out of the kindness of his heart. There was no documentation in his letters to explain why he chose to revamp the whole black school system. He seemed reticent to explain any motives for his altruism, preferring instead to stick to the nuts-and-bolts of implementation and construction in all his correspondence."

African-American students and their parents never looked into the "why" for Dupont's actions at that time, but they were very aware of what he did. Laura showed me letters written by children singing his praises. "Even though they may have been required to write them," said Laura, "you could tell they really liked what he had done for them. Some statements by the kids were, 'I will pay you back by being good and smart' and another said 'you'll never be sorry you gave these buildings to us.'"

DWIGHT MISSION SCHOOL, MARBLE CITY, OKLAHOMA. (Top right)
The Native American Dwight Mission School's dog-trot cabin is reconstructed from timbers saved from original buildings that once made up sections of the school.
BEAR MOUNTAIN MISSION SCHOOL, AMHERST COUNTY, VIRGINIA. (Bottom right)
The old log schoolhouse of the Bear Mountain Mission School, at the time of this photo, was undergoing renovation.

Dupont not only built the schools, but also made sure to have them well supplied with teaching material and, of most importance, qualified teachers. Dupont funded college scholarships for enterprising black students, hoping for some to return to the schools as teachers—most all the teachers in black schools were of color. Quality teaching did come to his schools. In the Iron Hill School, Laura told me of one teacher who had taught there: "The teacher was classically trained in ballet, and some of the students took lessons under her tutelage. She was also an accomplished pianist, so there was music and singing every day. These were not second-rate teachers by any means. Dupont made sure to put the resources into the schools to make sure they were successful."

By providing for the African-American community, Dupont was rewarded in knowing that after the schools were built and supplied, attendance jumped considerably. It validated Dupont's belief that if school buildings were nice, students would be more inclined to attend. During a school field trip, for example, some young students asked an elderly gentleman who had gone to Iron Hill School if he had cut classes. He told the students, "One day I pretended to be sick. By ten o'clock I was sorry I stayed home, and snuck over to the school to see what everyone was doing, but I didn't go in. In those days the teachers had hickory switches and they would use them on you if they thought you were pretending to be sick. Besides we all enjoyed going to school," he told the students. A lot of the past students told Laura that the school had a sense of com-

FREEMAN SCHOOL, BEATRICE, NEBRASKA.
Now part of Homestead National Monument, the brick Freeman School opened in 1872 and stopped classes in 1967. It is still on its original site.

munity, and when they closed it and started to bus the children to the bigger schools many parents fought a futile battle to keep it open. Black or white, these small schools were deeply loved.

Not all the benefactors to African-American education were white. A school in Atlanta, Louisiana, that I visited started with the donation of land, materials, and time from William Phillips and his wife Frances, African-Americans who had been born as slaves but later became prosperous enough to be large landowners. William was the local blacksmith and dentist for the community. They shared their good fortune with their neighbors by building not only the school, but also the Baptist church. The school is now on the National Register of Historic Places because the whole community valued the education they had received there and wanted to preserve its legacy by keeping it well maintained.

I had the incredible luck to arrive at the school around noon on a Sunday, when the service in the Baptist church next door was still in session. As the communicants exited the church I was able to talk my way into getting four past students to come over to the school, along with their minister, to tell me their school stories. Grace Clay was a bit younger than the rest of the group, and had gone to school here for only one year, as a preschooler. Her teacher that year was living with her family, and Clay vividly remembered walking to the school in the mornings with the teacher, holding her hand, as happy as she could be, because she was going to be learning new things and be with the older kids. She just loved the school. And in her expression,

FREEMAN SCHOOL, BEATRICE, NEBRASKA.
This view of the interior of the Freeman School looks over the teacher's desk toward the back of the room.

a wistful far-away look, one knew that the one year in the Phillips school has stayed powerfully in her memory all these years.

One of the best stories told came from Betty Washington. When she started to relate it to me, the rest of the group howled with laughter. Betty in her younger days was known for her love of boys and food (and she was not a big woman). "I was very small, what you call little, about ninety pounds, and I thought I was the queen of the crop when I came here. I would tease the boys a whole lot. I flirted real hard. I would always use flirting to get the boys' food. It is so funny now when I think of it, there were two brothers and they would always bring good food. They would have good biscuits, good squirrels, lots of baked potatoes, and I just loved it. I would just flirt with them." Here she paused a second then said, "and just get all their food—and eat!"

Shirley, another student, told of being the class cook and how Betty would always be at her side waiting for the food to be ready. Alex, in his very gentle way, told of only being able to go to the school until the sixth grade. He was the oldest of the group and felt the economic depression of those times more than the others. He had to go to work and earn money to help keep the family afloat. All felt that it was a good community school, with strong parental and community support. It showed, as the folks proudly told me of many past students having a successful adult life, with a fair amount of them having achieved college degrees.

As described earlier, one-room schoolhouses often served many purposes beyond simple education. When not functioning as a school, some became the local church with Sunday services. Social events, like Saturday night dances, wedding receptions, club meetings, and school plays all might take place in the school's single room, adding to the sense of community. It might have served as a town hall in a town with a small population, and in larger towns with multiple schools, it would serve as a regional, or mini, town hall, providing citizens with a polling place to cast their ballots, a dais for political debates, and a place to organize the citizens into political action groups.

The Freeman School, part of the Homestead National Monument in Beatrice, Nebraska, had many stories to tell and had a wonderful storyteller in Susan J. Cook, a park ranger and a native Nebraska daughter. An important court case involving separation of church and state began inside the walls of the classroom when a father of a student took issue with a teacher's use of the Bible for classroom instruction. Appeal after court appeal saw the case finally tried by the Nebraska State Supreme Court, which ruled in favor of the plaintiff, becoming a forerunner to church-state decisions later handed down by the U.S. Supreme Court. Another story I found fascinating was about gypsies. "The gypsies would come through town and camp close by," Susan related, "and they would send their children to the school to get an education until the sheriff, after a few months, would chase them all out of town. It would either double the size of the school or cut it in half overnight. Most times they would come back after a fashion and reenter their kids in the school again, and again be chased off—the life of a gypsy, I guess."

Another national monument of note is the Lyndon B. Johnson Ranch and Junction Schoolhouse. President Johnson, considered one of our most pro-education leaders, went to the Junction School for only a few months when he was four through special permission granted by teacher Miss Katie Deadrich.

Lyndon loved the school and liked to relate how he used to sit in her lap for his reading lessons. Later, as president, he signed one of the most important of his sixty education bills on the grounds of the school, accompanied by the still-active Miss Deadrich.

Neighbor states, Iowa and Missouri each have schools worth noting. The Goldenrod School in Iowa was where Jessie Field Shambaugh, a pioneer in the 4-H club movement, taught in 1901. Jessie started by creating farm and home courses for her students at the school and then expanding them into what became the 4-H clubs and camps. In a remote section of Missouri, in the vicinity of Indian Grove, north of Brunswick, "On a cold March night in the early 1900s, Aaron Bachtel called six of his neighbors together at the Newcomer Schoolhouse and organized the first farm club out of which the Missouri Farmers Association evolved," according to documents sent to me by Jeff Patridge of the State Historical Preservation Office. This organization was to be very tenacious in furthering the cause of the Missouri farmers. In a country so rich with farmland, but so controlled by mega-population centers, this group of individuals able to stand up for the plight of the farmers who provide our nation's bounty was a plucky and resolute body, organized, appropriately, in a rural one-room schoolhouse.

NEWCOMER SCHOOL, CHARITON COUNTY, MISSOURI. (Top) Within the Newcomer School local farmers gathered and founded the Missouri Farmers Association.
GOLDENROD SCHOOL, CLARIDON, IOWA. (Bottom left) The Goldenrod School is famous for being an early site in the development of the 4-H clubs.
JUNCTION SCHOOL, STONEWALL, TEXAS. (Bottom right) Beautifully clad in pressed tin, Junction School is now part of the Lyndon Baines Johnson National Historic Park. President Lyndon Johnson went here for a few months when he was four years old.

It was only natural that as populations grew in rural towns, the one-room schoolhouse would soon become claustrophobic. The solutions were to add other schoolhouses, expand present ones, or build new two-or-more-roomed structures. Some schoolhouses were first built big enough to be sectioned off inside into multiple rooms as needed, or could remain as one-roomers when school enrollment was low. Flexibility was necessary because of fluctuating local economies in areas with volatile industries like mining and ranching. Most of these schools would still have all the characteristics of a one-room school but were made more manageable with the addition of extra teachers. I could not resist including some of these structures as they reflected our explosive growth as a country.

**JUNCTION SCHOOL,
STONEWALL, TEXAS.**
Interior view of Junction
School—President Lyndon
Johnson told of sitting
on his teacher's lap while
she read to him here.

**CANTERBURY SHAKER SCHOOLHOUSE,
CANTERBURY, NEW HAMPSHIRE.** (Facing page)
(Top left and right) Though two stories high, the Canterbury
Shaker Schoolhouse schoolroom occupied only the upper floor.
(Bottom) Interior of the almost full-floor schoolroom.
**SCHOOLHOUSE AT HANCOCK SHAKER VILLAGE,
HANCOCK, MASSACHUSETTS.** (This page)
(Top left and right) The schoolhouse at Hancock Shaker Village,
next to other Shaker buildings.
(Bottom right) Interior of schoolroom. Note the letter boards
that were used in spelling games.

SAUM CONSOLIDATED AND OLD SAUM LOG SCHOOL, SAUM, MINNESOTA.
Here you can see the contrast of the original one-room log school and the larger consolidated school that later followed it. It was amazing they had the foresight to save the original log school.

RUGBY SCHOOLHOUSE, RUGBY, TENNESSEE.
Part of Historic Rugby, a utopian colony in eastern Tennessee begun in the 1880s, this building served as a school on the first floor and later as a church on the second floor.

COLUMBIA SCHOOL, COLUMBIA, CALIFORNIA.
(Left) Built in 1860, at a cost of $4,898, the two-story, two-room Columbia School stayed active until 1937, when it had to close because it did not meet the state's new earthquake codes. (Right) The classroom on the first floor of the Columbia School.

WYOMING VALLEY SCHOOL, WYOMING, WISCONSIN.
(Above) Just several miles south of Taliesen East, Frank Lloyd Wright's eastern home and studio, is the Wyoming school designed by Wright himself. The town hall to the left may have served as the one-room school prior to the Wright building.
(Top right) The school is typical of Frank Lloyd Wright's Prairie Style.
(Bottom right) Along with two classrooms the school had an auditorium room.

PENNSYLVANIA.
This active Amish one-room schoolhouse is in the middle part
of the state where there is a large Amish community.

Chapter Six

The One-Room Schoolhouse Today

SWEET BRIAR SCHOOL, SWEET BRIAR, NORTH DAKOTA.
Built in the mid-1920's by the WPA, this active schoolhouse in
immaculate condition was one of several Art Deco schoolhouses
that existed in the state.

In the preceding chapters one-room schools are discussed in the past tense—as if such institutions functioned only in the times of our parents, grandparents, and the many generations before them. What may come as a surprise is that many still exist and are still educating rural youth. To say they are thriving in rural America would be a big stretch—most kids today ride yellow buses—but yet, there are still pockets of one-room schools that are holding on and providing an educational experience very similar to what has been taking place for several hundred years, with the addition of such modern tools as computers and the Internet. Some of these schools are barely surviving, as state governments feel embarrassed by their existence and look for ways to eliminate them. Others are so isolated that there is no alternative to them. Finally, some special institutions, such as the Amish one-room schools, counter modern convention and continue to grow.

As I researched this project I selected six schools that are currently functioning. Three are traditional kindergarten through eighth grade schools. They are represented geographically across the United States: the central part of the country, in North Dakota; the West Coast, in California; and the East Coast, in Maine. The other schools, while not as comprehensive, utilize the traditional one-room schoolhouse. Two, Grandville in Vermont and Prudence Island in Rhode Island, include kindergarten through fourth grade, while Wainscott on Long Island teaches first through third grades. All have unique stories to tell and all provided me some of the most memorable experiences of my thirty-three years in photography.

Sweet Briar School, Sweet Briar, North Dakota

The dirt road that leads to Sweet Briar School is a comfortable two-lane path. I pulled off the highway and had become one with the landscape. It was in direct contrast to the highway, with its four lanes, medians, breakdown lanes, and side acreage along the road, all of which separates you from the landscape, the farms, and the terrain. On back roads the landscape envelops you. Off the interstate you see the farms settle into low rolling hills, protected from the wind by 100- to 200-foot hills. In this part of the country there are not many trees. When you see them, they are in pockets, set like the farms in sheltered areas, seemingly huddled together against the elements.

The sky is the essence of this land—as you turn 360 degrees, the sky is surrounding you. If you look up quickly the sky looks high, but if you look at it from the horizon and slowly bring your eyes to the zenith, it seems to press down like a big blue inverted saucer. A high ridge a mile to the south of the school conceals it from a visitor approaching from the north. But once over the hill, standing out in the landscape, especially on a sunny day, is the brilliant white of the Sweet Briar School, along with the flag fluttering in an almost constant breeze.

Teacher Toni Wheeler has an easy demeanor. Her classroom style is marked by a constant flow through a reserved but friendly personality. She is well dressed, attractive, young, and a very new mother. I was curious about how her kids responded to the pregnancy during the spring term when she was really showing. I need not have wondered, as these were farm kids who were in tune with the developments of nature, seeing all of its possibilities through the lives of their farm animals. They took their teacher's pregnancy in stride but were extremely anxious to see the baby as soon as they could.

Born in North Dakota and raised in Miles City, Montana, Toni did not attend a one-room school as a youth. Her family did, though, and some—her father, grandmother, and great aunt—taught in them. They were the ones who encouraged her to take the job when it opened up six years ago. In response to my question about whether her teacher training had prepared her for this kind of work, she responded, "No, you pretty much jump in, and survive or sink. Help came from my supervisor, Karen Kautzmann." (It should be noted that Karen Kautzmann is the daughter-in-law of Mrs. Avis Kautzmann, who was previously profiled.) "She referred me to former teachers and a few who were still actively teaching in reduced-grades one-room schools." ("Reduced grades" refers to schools that teach only from kindergarten to the fourth grade.) "I had classrooms of thirty students, all one grade, prior to Sweet Briar," she explains, "and I thought, well, it will be pretty hectic but it should be easier going down to sixteen. That wasn't the case. For one thing, we have very cramped quarters—you have to fit all the desks and everybody into a very small room. It was also difficult at first trying to prepare for all those grades and making sure that they were getting the best education possible. Because your time is so limited you can't spend it with a single grade for the whole day like you would at a regular school. I guess the hardest part was managing my time so that each group would feel like they received their lessons and learned the material. But I soon realized that the kids take on a lot of responsibility themselves—they are very responsible. They have a part in organizing their own lessons that makes it a lot easier on me. I didn't have to plan as I would in a bigger school because of their independence. They plan themselves and know what assignment is coming next. They know when their test is going to be without my having to prompt them."

During my trip, I had heard from so many people about how multiple-age classroom tends to foster eavesdropping on what grades above and below were doing. Since these stories all preceded my visit to a current one-roomer, I was curious if the pattern also applied to today. "Kids listen to the other grades," Toni said. "As an example, my youngest kindergarten student four years ago never wanted to stay in her grade. She constantly wanted to listen to what the other kids were doing. She was eager to advance. Although I made her do her assigned level work, I did allow her to forge ahead in the higher grade book when she had her free time, because that was her own time to choose. She chose to do that instead of working on the computer or playing games, and sometimes she would take the material home and study it as if it were her own. Last year she was interested in science and got very interested in the eighth-grade science book. Fascinated with the material, she studied hard and took the same tests as my eighth-grade girls. She was pulling A minuses and B pluses, and embarrassing the eighth graders with their sometimes C grades when they had slackened on their studying. I told her parents, 'I don't know how I'm going to keep her in her own books this year.'"

I couldn't help but think, Boy, a teacher's nightmare, a student who really wants to learn! Toni told me that this girl and another girl one grade higher watch her like hawks when she is teaching, to pick up hints on what she is doing to get her message across to the students. Why? Because they help out the first- and second-graders, acting like miniature teachers, reading to them, helping with their spelling, and just

SWEET BRIAR SCHOOL, SWEET BRIAR, NORTH DAKOTA.
Class in session with Mrs. Wheeler (top row) and assistant teacher Diane Kuether (middle row, left). The older students helping the younger ones in their studies is a typical scene.

being available as problem solvers. Anyone who has ever taught will know that you really learn your material when you have to relate it intelligently to someone else. In the case of these "junior teachers," since they have just learned the material, they are more attuned to the difficulties of comprehension than a teacher light years away from the struggles going on in young brain cells.

I had the chance to ask the two girls about the "competition" they were giving Toni as a teacher. "It is fun," said Shelby, "they look up to you when you help them. They kind of want to be like you."

Kaley added, "It is fun, and it makes you feel important." That was not said in an arrogant way but as an expression of the self-esteem that was building as a result of helping others to succeed and to become a part of the success of the whole. I could not help but think how much more difficult that might be in a standard graded school, with teachers more prone to feel challenged by students wanting to help teach other students. In Toni's class, and all others that I visited, the older students were expected to help out the younger ones. It was expected that a close cooperation between those in the same grade would exist. This pattern mimics a good family situation where the old Three Musketeers motto, "all for one, and one for all" prevailed. In the busyness of a one-room school, with teachers dealing with so many grades, success depends on delegating some teaching responsibility to students; responsibility makes for responsibility.

Parents with any sense of concern for their children's education are the most critical and demanding of the professional educational system. I could talk to the teachers, and they could be honest or not; supervisors could be locked into narrowly thought out educational philosophies—but with parents, you could

expect more of a straight answer. As parents arrived to the school to pick up their children, I was able to talk with those who had the time, and I was able to receive opinions from two mothers with active students.

Heidi Gress has a sixth grader at the school. She felt if her son Cullen attended a bigger school he would not enjoy the same close friendships that he has at Sweet Briar, not only with his own age group, but also with children older and younger than him. Heidi also felt that by listening to older classes he could pay attention to what materials were coming. Repetition from younger class levels, on the other hand, helped cement Cullen's lessons. Heidi also commented on the exceptional one-on-one attention she felt the teacher gave the students. These positives were not a recent phenomenon. Heidi told me, "My husband and his five siblings went to school here and they were none the worse for it. They are all very successful in life. My husband has warm memories of going to school here, like the Halloween parties and the haunted house they got to create. He says it was like going through school as a family"—the family being the extended family of all the children.

Diane Bosworth, another parent, had this to say about her children. "My kids like to go to school—actually they want to go to school." She continued, "My older son in high school is on the honor roll and the National Honor Society—whatever happened while going here was good for him. I have had comments from his high school teachers that he is ahead of children who went through a normal consolidated school."

Karen Kautzmann is the superintendent of two school districts with a total of ten schools, of which Sweet Briar is one. Diane Bosworth's comment came up when I interviewed Karen, and she responded, "I was at a legislative hearing on a bill to do away with all the small rural schools. They had a lot of speakers in protest to the bill from small schools throughout the state, including Sweet Briar. Each of them had examples of test scores from their schools and compared them to test scores from the larger district schools. The one-room scores either exceeded the district schools' or compared favorably to them." The speakers, many who were students, continued their argument for retaining the rural schools, some one-room, with most being smaller two- to four-room schools. "They also brought out that when they graduated to the high school level they were the types who received merit scholarships and other awards of educational excellence," Karen explained. In hers and other school-district studies, it was shown that rural school students do very well in high school and are quite prepared to attend college by the end of their senior year.

One may ask, "Why close them?" For one thing, they are not always cost-effective. Running a school with fewer than ten students is more expensive than busing students to a school at another site. But that site may be far away, and parents may not want their kids riding for excessive times on buses, so they will sometimes protest when the school district wants to shut down a local rural school. As another school supervisor, Steven L. Johnson, told me, "Parents like to have their children going to school close by to where they work. It makes it easier for them, especially with after-school activities."

Parents in many rural schools like Sweet Briar feel their school is more like family. The relationships are close, and they do not want to do away with that; it is too important to them. At the same legislative hearing, a proponent of keeping the schools open asked if a school district wanted to keep a school open, even though it was going to raise local taxes and the community was willing to pay the extra, would the legislature be willing to keep the school open. A quick answer from one ranking member was affirmative. I asked Karen how she felt about keeping these schools open, in particular Sweet Briar, because all those connected to the school wanted it to continue. "I am a big proponent of keeping Sweet Briar as it is," she responded. "What I see as the chief advantage of Sweet Briar is that it has had wonderful, dedicated, and competent teachers for all its lifetime. And that, for me, is the key to quality education. It takes precedence over time and money. If you have quality teachers in this type of setting you can excel."

Karen also confirmed my observation that teaching in the school is not always through the teachers. She noted, "I have found that at times teaching can come from another student in a higher grade. Students are more apt, at times, to want to work with a student closer to their own age. They don't feel so stigmatized. Help can feel less threatening coming from a fellow student than from a teacher."

In terms of the average day's schedule at Sweet Briar, here was what I observed. It is presumptuous to make an evaluation of a school on the basis of two days of observations. What I picked up on might have been just a singular happenstance, or it might be fully accurate. I take some reservations to what I portray. But in defense of my observations, most of the positive things I saw, most of it had been corroborated by other sources.

The morning begins with a group discussion of what has happened since school let out the previous day. Family happenings, regional, country, and world events are discussed, with all encouraged to participate. The older students are more in tune with events beyond the town and the younger ones with events that took place on their farms and homes and with friends and siblings. The younger students are cautioned to respect and listen to the older students, and the older students show manners in listening to the very self-oriented stories of the tots. With the end of discussion the students break into class groups more in line with their grade levels. Toni's assistant on my first day met with the first and second graders, and on my second day Toni met with them. Whoever is not having direct contact with a teacher is expected to be working on a project or helping out a student or students solve problems on which they have more experience and knowledge. That can also mean reading to the lower grades. (These kids are all good readers and seem to devour books that are available to bring home.)

At mid-morning, recess is called. When the children go outdoors Toni mandates that the first part of recess is some game that is played as a total class, to enhance school team spirit. The older students are very patient with the younger ones, despite their smaller physical size. After the prescribed game, the kids break up into more clearly defined age groups. Still, I watched older boys take the time for a pick-up game with first and second graders. Also, I saw no bullying anywhere. The older students did not get bullied when they were tots and they have not introduced it now. Also, I think if they did that, their peers would chastise them, and some of those peers are the older brothers and sisters of the littler kids. Resources for recess equipment are limited, so there is a great deal of improvising games and equipment. Stones, sticks, and natural obstacles, all are fodder for creative minds in devising games to play while outdoors.

After the allotted time, all return inside with a chosen student ringing the school bell. Study groups re-emerge, and Toni and her assistant move on to teach other groupings while some grade levels work on pre-scribed projects or take tests. Lunch time finds the kids devouring their food quickly so they can go out and play or just hang out, talking the talk of youth. In the afternoon the morning cycle repeats itself with class time, recess, and more class time. First and second graders need more attention because of their youth. The upper-graders Shelby and Kaley would, during the afternoon when young ones get more restless, read to them as soon as they had completed their own work.

At the end of the day, work stops ten minutes short of the prescribed time of dismissal so the children can clean the room. All have specific jobs, which rotate as much as they can considering the age and dexterity of the students. There is a bit of lingering after school ends, with the students socializing with each other or talking with the teachers about things they might not have had time to go over during class. Being a serious clock-watcher in my grammar school days I was amazed by their willingness to hang around school, given what I would have considered the opportunity to escape the premises. The kids really seem to like the place. They also seem to be very fond of both Toni and her assistant; it was an environment that worked very well for them. Even I, one of New York City's least motivated students while growing up, liked the place and felt I might have enjoyed going to school there.

Mt. Hamilton School, Mt. Hamilton, California

The Mt. Hamilton school was started in 1898 for the workmen's families and scientists who would be sta-

MT. HAMILTON SCHOOL, MT. HAMILTON, CALIFORNIA.
(Top) The school is nestled into the side of the hill and is surrounded by the multiple Lick observatories.
(Bottom left) Teacher Patricia Ann Graham (seated) and her assistant Sheryl Severinsen (standing).
(Bottom right) Interior of classroom.

tioned at Lick Astronomical Observatory at the top of Mt. Hamilton. The road up to the school begins at the very eastern edge of San Jose and winds its way, with switchbacks and hairpin turns, up the Diablo mountain range to the protruding peak of Mt. Hamilton. Unfortunately, not paying the closest attention to directions, I needed assistance from a couple of road workers. Luckily, after another half-hour of curves and hairpin turns, I made my way to the school. (Later, I was to find out that those who commute, either to Mt. Hamilton or the reverse way to San Jose, spend an inordinate amount of money on brakes and tires during the course of a year because of the road's unforgiving condition.) The agonizing drive was more than worth it when I reached the peak and an incredibly beautiful vista. The school nestled in with the multiple observatories gave an impression of being on an island at the top of the world.

The school still exists today because of the road I traveled on. One might think that nobody in his or her right mind would want to subject little children to the daily hazards of crossing such a narrow path, not to mention the two-hour round trip commute to a consolidated school in San Jose. However, rational decisions are not always made. Pat Graham, the school's teacher, and her assistant, Sheryl Severinsen, are now down to five students. Grades represented are first, second, third, fourth, and eighth. The school is holding on tenuously to its existence; with fewer than five students it becomes subject to closure. Pat has done her part to increase enrollment by talking with families living in the mountain towns and asking them to send their children to her school. There used to be other one-room schools in the mountains, but they have closed due to low enrollment. There have been some children available to transfer to Pat's school and to keep it going; Pat thinks and hopes that more children will be coming of school age next year, when she loses her eighth grader to high school.

Pat has come up with an interesting idea to keep the numbers up: She uses computers as a virtual extension of classroom space. If she could interest some parents in the valley in registering their children at Mt. Hamilton while allowing them to work out of their homes or in special classrooms in a consolidated school in San Jose, she possibly could count those children in her attendance levels. They would be tied in to Mt. Hamilton through a powerful computer hook-up and only have to make the trip up to the school one or two days a week.

It had been a week or so since my time at Sweet Briar, so comparisons between the schools were fresh in my mind. As with the Sweet Briar teachers, I found Pat and Sheryl to be very competent and involved teachers. The lower enrollment and the one older student did change the dynamics of the class, though. Pat and Sheryl taught the students more directly since there were fewer class levels to worry about. The younger students could be grouped more easily, and the older boy usually received more personal attention from Pat or Sheryl as there was no one of his age group with whom to share knowledge. If Pat and Sheryl could hold on for another year or two, the increased ratio of older to younger students would allow for more cross-teaching.

If there are any problems with modern-day one-room schools, it is a shortage of students to make the machinery hum as at full enrollment. Even so, Pat said, "David, my eighth grader, acts like a big brother to the younger children. They look up to him." Pat was most passionate about one-room schools. The subject of her master's thesis was one-room-school education.

She felt that to have a successful one-room school you have to have an involved and supportive community. As she told me, "My goal is to make the school the heart of the community because that is what a one-room school is all about. The one-room school was and, in many places, still is the glue that holds a community together. Young or old, rich or poor, married or single, children or no children, the school can draw out the best in a community in support of the education of future generations."

Pat's fight was with the concept of "bigger is better," where many students are gathered so there are many children in each grade level. She felt the challenge of preparing for multiple grades was a positive thing. "Teachers in a one-room school can't teach the same thing year after year because you have the same kids listening in for several years," she said. "It makes you constantly look for different ways of approaching the material. I think that is a plus. I know it keeps me learning." Pat also felt that the one-room school is conducive to helping students with learning problems. She related a story of one child who had come up from San Jose and who had not been functioning as well as he could have in the larger schools. Within the atmosphere of the open multiple-age one-roomer at Mt. Hamilton, the child started to mature and become an excellent learner. It was to everyone's sadness that he could only spend one year at Mt. Hamilton. The teachers hoped the changes that took place while there would follow him along as he went back to regular schools. Discussion of this student led Pat to state to me her educational philosophy: "To create lifelong learners and not just kids who know the answers." I pondered over these final words as I wound my way back down to the valley floor.

Isle Au Haut School, Isle Au Haut, Maine

Sandwiching the visits to Sweet Briar and Mt. Hamilton were two trips to Isle au Haut school in Maine. While Mt. Hamilton was an "island in the sky" in the coastal mountains of California, Isle Au Haut, some 3,000 miles away, was a real island surrounded by the waters of Penobscot Bay. In mid-October I heard about a one-room school on the island, and when I happened to be nearby stopped by for an unannounced visit. I did not expect much from the teacher on this trip but planned to return in December if I liked the school. Fortunately, though we had in effect barged in, teacher Judy Jipson was very cordial and accommodating. Even luckier, a biologist from Acadia National Park, a section of which is on Isle au Haut, had come from Bar Harbor that day to give a talk to the students. Having time available, Judy graciously allowed us to interview her while her students were learning coastal biology in the basement.

Isolation is an appropriate word for life here, at least for the majority of the year. Each summer generations of families return to the island where they have built homes to escape the stress of metropolitan living. Also, with a slice of Acadia National Park on the island, during the nice months many day-trippers come on the ferry to take advantage of the beautiful hiking trails circling the island. When late autumn arrives and all the transients have gone, Isle au Haut is left with roughly fifty permanent residents. Almost all of them are involved with the harvest of lobsters from the bountiful lobstering grounds around the island. For the full-time residents, summer is busy with lobstering and winter weather creates a tough ferry ride, so going to the mainland is reserved for essential trips, like stocking up on groceries, going for medical visits, or relieving serious cases of cabin

ISLE AU HAUT SCHOOL, ISLE AU HAUT, MAINE.
Morning brings a new school day to this Classical-styled
schoolhouse.

fever. If you live and work on the island, you tend to stay on the island.

Teacher Judy Jipson and her husband have lived on Isle au Haut for several years now. She has developed a wonderful grasp of the island and its people and compliments them on the support they give to the education of the island's children. That support comes not only from the year-round residents but also from the seasonal visitors. "We have a big summer population," Judy said. "We do fund-raisers during the warm months, and the summer people generously donate money that goes towards maintaining the school and providing field trips for the children." The field trip funds are supplemented by local and state educational funds, with outings scheduled on a monthly basis for all the children. Being isolated as they are, the children need to be exposed to mainland culture—high and low—as often as possible, Judy feels. This adapts the children to a world they may choose to live in after high school graduation. Most of the field trips last only one day, but longer ones are also scheduled. Judy said she has taken the children on weeklong trips to such places as Washington, D.C., Gettysburg, and Philadelphia. "All the kids go on these trips because it is so important to them," Judy emphasized.

It is also important to acclimatize the higher grades to the transition into high school in Stonington, on the mainland. High school, with changing classes, lockers, a cafeteria, a gym, and many more students, can be intimidating to an island student used to the comforting confines of a one-room school. As Judy noted, "Where they have had only me, they will have six different teachers." Island isolation for children has to be alleviated when they get to high school age, so Judy sets the wheels in motion. She began a program where her eighth graders go to Stonington's eighth-grade class twice a month and meet other kids who will be in their high school classes. This gives them a chance to make friends with other students, and to ease the difficult transition from grade school to high school.

Judy told us of her special preparation for teaching in a one-room school. First, she became certified to teach kindergarten to eighth grade. She is also certified to teach special-needs children from kindergarten through twelfth grade. She takes classes whenever she can to keep abreast of current trends in education. These classes give her a chance to talk with other teachers, something she says is difficult to do isolated on the island. Once a year, teachers from all the Maine islands come together to talk about related matters. Other than that, Judy is on her own, though with the help and encouragement of her teaching assistant, Lisa Turner. She does miss the camaraderie with other teachers that takes place in a regular school, where ideas and problems can be tossed about during the day for discussion and solutions. But she also said that she loves the island and the school, and plans to be there awhile.

Judy explained some concepts of classroom teaching that are not found in normal consolidated schools with individual grades, but which work well in a multi-age class. First and foremost was her belief that success was directly tied to knowing the needs of each individual student. "In my first year here, I know I had never worked harder. I was trying to know what the needs of the students were, then to meet those needs in ways that were best for them. The emphasis on individual attention forced me to look at my curriculum and make adaptations as circumstances presented themselves."

Taking the teaching of social studies as an example, she told me how she structures these classes for all the grades. She arranges the students in three groups:

group one—kindergarten and first and second grades; group two—third, fourth, and fifth grades; and group three—sixth, seventh, and eighth grades. She divides the subject into three-year loops. The first year covers Maine history; the second year, U.S. history; and the third year, world history. As children progress to higher grade levels they move up to the next three-year loop, which is structured the same but at a higher level of intensity. Thus, by the time they have finished eighth grade they will have gone through three three-year loops. Judy also uses this looping technique with the science units. With three grade levels traveling through each loop, three age levels are working together in a manner that fosters cooperation between younger and older students. In what she calls "math manipulative," this idea is taken even further by doing daily math games, where she can have a second grader sometimes paired with an eighth grader.

As at Sweet Briar and Mt. Hamilton, the integration of grades is part of the teaching structure and is used to make the whole larger than any single unit, producing a cohesiveness of purpose as a group. Within this group concept is the appreciation of individual talent. As Judy said, "I have an eighth grader doing high school algebra, a second grader doing third-grade math, and a sixth grader at the seventh-grade math level. It depends on their needs and their abilities with each subject." Using her teaching units, math manipulative, and open advancement to higher grade levels, Judy allows for a more dynamic and fresh class environment. Being with the same children for such a long period of time, though, it is imperative that they do not hear an undue amount of repetition. "It would be very boring to the children to hear the same thing over and over. I have to be very careful not to do that to them."

After hearing her expound on the island, the school, and her one-room teaching experiences, I knew I had to come back. Little did I know I was going to be treated to a special play on my return. I arrived on the island in late December, before Christmas vacation. This school day was going to be a bit different from most and it had nothing to do with my being in attendance. In fact, I told them, as I told all the other schools I photographed, to ignore my presence and just go about their normal business. The first half of the day proceeded as usual. First on the academic agenda was a book report given by Brianna Devereux, a second grader, to the whole class, followed by another book report by eighth-grader Kyle Devereux (Brianna's older brother) in partnership with seventh-grader Waylan Small. Each had to read the same book and give a solo report, while teaming up for the major part of the presentation.

The focus of the middle part of the morning was on academic activities, with the children grouped according to logical age and scholastic levels. With a total of six students—one in second grade, one in fourth grade, two in fifth grade, and one each in seventh and eighth grades—the children were broken up into age-appropriate groups, which would rotate. During each rotation, Judy would work with one group, Lisa with another, and the third would work on an assigned project by themselves. With the individual attention Judy and Lisa were able to give each child, problems the children might have grasping subject matter could be addressed quickly and effectively. When they worked

(Top Left) View of Isle au Haut as the ferry leaves the harbor.
(Top Right) The two older boys collaborated on a board game to illustrate their book project.
(Bottom Left) Dress rehearsal for the Christmas play.
(Bottom Right) The cloak room doubles as a cozy reading room.

without the teachers' direct involvement they were encouraged to help each other with any problems that arose in learning new material.

Late in the morning the music teacher arrived for the students' music session. Though the predominantly blue-collar Isle au Haut does not have a reputation for the arts, especially as compared with Monhegan Island, the arts colony forty miles across the open mouth of Penobscot Bay, a few permanent residents have creative talents that they enthusiastically share with the students. The music teacher is one, and she comes in on a regular basis to provide a music program for the school. Today was special because she, Judy, Lisa, and the kids were preparing for the night's Christmas play. It was to include a musical recital by all students and the performance of a play based on The Grinch Who Stole Christmas. It was an exciting time for the children as they honed their skills on their instruments.

Lunch followed music. Then, even in the cold of December, the kids went outside after lunch to burn off some youthful energy. With the ringing of the school bell all were back inside gathering props, costumes, and all the needs for the night's performance at the town hall, a short distance down the road in the direction of the harbor. The children walked to the town hall, eager to decorate and prepare the interior for their parents' arrival in the evening.

I took the opportunity to walk with eighth grader Kyle. He and his sister had recently moved to the island from Florida. The contrast seemed extreme. He said, "It felt a little strange, at first, coming into this situation after being in a consolidated school, but I felt I would get used to it quickly." He found more individual attention was given here, and it helped him resolve problems in a couple of subjects. He was able to bring his grades up to a B plus from a C minus. That occurred even with tougher academic standards than he had in Florida. Though he missed having more friends his age, he was enjoying living on the island and felt very grateful to Mrs. Jipson for the excellent and interesting education he was receiving.

I had not seen a school play since my own kids were in grammar school. In a few short years, I will have the opportunity to relive those early experiences with my grandchildren. But until then I will have in my mind the wonderful performance all six kids put on during their dress rehearsal that afternoon. On the ferry back to Stonington, I was imagining their parents, relatives, and friends beaming with pride during what is one of the most anticipated potluck dinners and school performances of the year.

Grandville Village School, Grandville, Vermont

"I love the history of the building. It is wonderful to know that when Lincoln was president children were coming in here to do the same thing we are doing today," said Peter Flaherty, the third and fourth grade teacher of Grandville Village School. This small New England town, nestled in a narrow valley created by the headwaters of the White River, is about as centrally located as you can get in Vermont. Grandville is a blue-collar town where the residents scratch out a living in the forest trades, at the ski areas in the winter, and tourist-related endeavors during the summer months. It is a cute town, but not one of your picturesque Vermont gems filled with stately eighteenth- and nine-

GRANDVILLE VILLAGE SCHOOL, GRANDVILLE, VERMONT. (Clockwise from top left) Singing with music teacher Carol Cronce. Teacher Charlotte Holmquist with grades K-2 in the town hall (next three). Peter Flaherty uses his dynamic teaching methods on grades 3 and 4 (next three). Exterior of Grandville School and town hall, both used for teaching.

teenth-century houses circling a town green. The school and town-hall complex is a lovely exception, being quite charming. While I was there, during the height of the fall foliage season, I noticed many "leaf-peepers" stopping their cars to photograph the buildings.

In strictest terms, Grandville School cannot be considered a one-room school. Its classes are held in two separate areas: third and fourth grade in the old school building, and kindergarten through second grade in the town hall. Each grouping has its own teacher. In principle, however, the school represents the best in one-room schooling philosophy. All the grades get together for activities several times a day, there is cross-learning between grades, and the teachers subscribe to a looser interpretation of grade levels, allowing individual students flexibility in their progress. The morning I arrived, I encountered a group activity immediately. All the children were around the piano in the town hall, singing songs.

"I just love teaching here," said Peter, as he moved from table to table among his third and fourth graders. "Coming here from teaching in a big-city school in Minneapolis was a breath of fresh air." I do not know how much Irish was in Peter Flaherty, but it came through loud and clear with his theatrical presentation style and impish offbeat humor. He kept the kids both laughing and on their toes as they learned. He was well aware of what he was doing, as I found out later when I asked if he would like to stretch the school into the fifth grade. "I have only so many tricks up my sleeve and corny jokes to use up," he responded. "To put a kid through a third year of me would be cruel and unusual punishment."

In contrast, Charlotte Holmquist, the kindergarten-to-second-grade teacher, conveyed a more subdued style, though she clearly maintained a good rapport with her students. As I photographed her with her three grades in the town hall section, her deliberate and firm manner was neutralizing the natural squirminess and shorter attention span of the very young students in her groups. They were getting her message that playtime was for recess, class time was for lessons, and she kept their attention. She was aware that she and Peter had very different teaching styles, and said as much when we were all together for the interview. Both teachers understood each other and saw their different approaches as complements rather than as sources of contention. Peter said he heard a few parents tell their children about their days in the school when it last had one teacher: "Boy, you kids are lucky to have Mr. Flaherty and Mrs. Holmquist. It was really tough with the teachers back when we were going here." Of course, it is common for parents to comment on the contrasts of their children's living conditions with what they remember having to go through as youths, but in this case there may be real differences.

The Grandville Village School was my first experience with a modified one-room school as an alternative to consolidation. It emphasizes one-room teaching philosophies in the very critical first five years of education. Others existed, such as Wainscott School in outer Long Island. What were their reasons for maintaining the one-room system? Foremost was the belief that one-room schools worked and worked well. Charlotte said, "The one-room school is probably the best education one can have, and I regret that my own children did not go here. They went to a bigger school, and I have seen gaps in their education that could have been corrected by more individualized attention."

Explaining the reason for the two-teacher adaptation at Grandville, Peter noted, "We are expected to cover so much these days that meeting the needs of the kindergartner through highest fourth grader, and everything in between, is more than any one person should be asked to try."

Since Grandville is not as isolated as the three previous schools profiled, both teachers felt that by fifth grade the students needed to move on to a bigger school. "By the time they get to fifth grade they need a bigger social pond to swim in, just to meet new kids and have experiences with new teachers," Peter explained.

A new kindergarten student just happened to be spending his first few days in the school during my visit. Since they were well into the fall session, it could only mean that the boy's family was a new arrival in town. What could be the reaction of new people to finding that their child would be attending a one-room school? "Sometimes they are surprised to find that a school like this still exists," said Peter. "Most are thrilled by it. They are going to see their children develop a closer relationship with a teacher—given eighteen students attended to by two teachers and incoming aids and specialists. In a multi-graded classroom their child will also get more opportunity for peer coaching and tutoring."

Charlotte added, "Getting away from the rigidity of grades allows us to concentrate more on the level of each individual child."

"And as our motto on our Web site says," Peter informed me, "'The best in one room.' We try to offer the best education these kids can get. We think that doing it in a small group setting like this gives them limitless opportunities."

Was a school like this as vulnerable to closure as the full-scale one-roomers? The consensus was that there was no pressure yet to close the school even though the state was looking to have more schools consolidated. Local control had such a big part to play in

Vermont that as long as the town was willing to pay what it cost, these types of schools would continue. Charlotte believed the residents still liked having the school located in town. "They feel more in control with it here," Peter added. "It would be more impersonal to have them bused to Rochester. The parents value having them close by and being close to the education they are having."

Both told me a quote from one mother who had moved in from a larger town: "Coming here is like coming home." The extended home atmosphere was very gratifying to parents, especially when their kids were in the early grades. This was something I felt in all the schools I visited. In the bigger schools, if you wanted to visit the classroom you had to go through an office, but in these schools you came right into your child's classroom. It seemed to be more comforting for everyone.

Prudence Island School, Prudence Island, Rhode Island

When I first talked to Vicky Flaherty over the phone I knew any relationship between her and Peter Flaherty from Grandville Village School would be remote, at best, since the accent coming over the wires indicated a Southern upbringing—deep Southern. We were to meet on the ferry from Bristol to Prudence Island since she was a mainlander with a thirty-minute commute each morning to the island's school. It was while we were on the ferry one blustery, frigid morning in early January that I learned how an Alabama lady became located in Rhode Island and began to teach in a one-room school. I was instantly mesmerized with her stories and Southern charm. She had found her way to Rhode Island by way of an air show she had attended in the area several years back. It was there that she met a fellow aeronautical enthusiast, started a

romance, and prepared to marry the gentleman. Commuting from Gadsden, Alabama, was out of the question, so she looked for a teaching position in the area, and as the big day came close she received a call from the search committee about a job on Prudence Island, teaching in a one-room schoolhouse. The interview for the job was at the end of the week on Saturday. Excited about the idea, she told them she would love to interview but was getting married that same day at one o'clock on Rose Island (a beautiful little island that overlooks Newport). "When they said I could be the first interview at nine o'clock, I said, 'Let's do it.' During the interview, they were saying I would have to take a ferry to work every morning, and I said, 'I'm taking one this afternoon to get married.' I think I showed them dedication by showing up on my wedding day, and in having no fear of ferries. I got the job."

Later at the wedding she told her family about interviewing for a job teaching in a one-room schoolhouse. "That is so like you," they said. "I'm adventuresome. I taught at a space school in Siberia for a period of time." Positive reactions to Vicky's unique teaching situation are quite common when they make their way into conversation. One type of gathering where conversations run rampant, especially about education, are teachers' conferences. Vicky's bubbly personality at these conferences effervesces with stories about Prudence Island School and what it is like to teach there. Colleagues in education are a rapt audience, gathering around her wanting to know more about the experience and teaching conditions. They are fasci-

PRUDENCE ISLAND SCHOOL, PRUDENCE ISLAND, RHODE ISLAND. (Clockwise from top left) The children arrive for the school day. Teacher Vicky Flaherty explains a point in her student's workbook. Computer time with assistant Elizabeth Howland. Mrs. Flaherty and students engaged in a learning game.

nated by the concept of a one-room school in this day and age. "I tell them that it is like a big happy family there. The kids are very supportive of each other, and if a student does something well they all will brag about it. They are not usually competitive with each other, but looking to be helpful if someone needs it. So much is shared between the students." As with the other teachers I interviewed, Vicky's experiences in a standard one-grade class involved a disproportionate amount of time keeping order in the class. So, at the conferences she ends her stories with the coup de grace: "I have no discipline problems! They think I am the luckiest teacher around, and want to trade places with me." Positive behavior begins when the kindergarten and first graders first come to school. "They learn so much from the older students who take a sense of responsibility of being good examples. The younger children want to emulate them. The normal dynamics of childish behavior and sibling rivalry change when the kids step into the room, but definitely reappear when outside the confines of the school ground. I know, I have seen it on the ferry going on field trips. These really are normal kids." Vicky wanted me to talk to her fourth grader, Roy Shaw, whom she said was pretty erudite for his age and who had given strong interviews in the past. By the time I was ready to talk to him I had watched the class dynamics for several hours while photographing the activities of the day. I can vouch for the claims he made of his class involvement.

"My five years here have been very exciting and probably very different from other schools. I've liked all the attention I've gotten from the teacher. We are very flexible here. I could have easily gotten lost in a bigger school. We go on a lot of field trips, which I love. A real cool one was a kids' science museum. It was so exciting and fun; you were learning things and not really realizing it." I mentioned to him how I watched his involvement with the younger students, and he said, "It is fun to read to the little kids. Sometimes you get to help them with their assignments if the teachers are busy. It has been fun to watch them grow up and learn." I detected a sense of wistfulness in his voice. I asked him how he felt about leaving here at the end of the year. "I know I'll have to adjust. There will be more people, I'll have to make new friends, and learn how to get around a bigger building. I'll miss this school." There was a prediction of a winter storm coming in the evening, and I had a four-hour journey to get back home. Vicky had told me that Roy's father ran a water taxi that could take me back across the bay to my car three hours before the ferry could, so I took advantage of it. While crossing over, Mr. Shaw told me of the wonderful qualities the school had from a parent's point of view: "In the big school across the bay it is hard to know the teacher. Vicky is a personal friend of ours, we are on a first-name basis, and if we need to speak to her we just call her on the phone to say we are coming in. You really have a one-on-one with her." He was also a strong proponent of the multi-age concept. "When you have kids older than you, helping you, you pick up the material easier. If there was some way to get something like our school on the mainland into their curriculum, their students would learn so much faster." I realized then I had not heard, in all the schools I visited, a parent who said they did not like the education their child was getting in a one-room schoolhouse.

Wainscott School, Wainscott, Long Island, New York
It is story-time for the children. They are clustered in front of their schoolmarm, Julie Medler, who is seated in a big wooden rocking chair in a school that has been around for more than 270 years in an old farming community in outer Long Island. Julie is an attractive young blond teacher who in a calm but dynamic way teaches a progressive first to third grade one-room school in Wainscott, Long Island, which is surrounded by the tony communities of Southampton, Bridgehampton, and East Hampton. The school is located in what would have been central access to the farms of yesteryear. Some farms are still working, with the old farming community holding on as best they can. But the relentless pressure to convert farmland to residential land to build second homes here has sown the seeds of change, with the spring bringing more building foundations out of the ground than vegetable crops. The year-rounders still have control over the school and they do not want to see it change any more than it has to. And as Julie said emphatically to me, "It is a good school . . . Many people like our philosophy of the multi-age, all-in-one-room concept. It has always been the philosophy of this school to teach to the children's ability instead of to very strict grade levels. Each child has more of an individualized education that way." In a small school like Wainscott, the teacher also has the flexibility to adapt the curriculum to the group's needs as well, though Julie still manages to match the New York State learning standards very closely. I also live in an area that is a retreat from New York City for the elite of business and culture. Since September 11, 2001, I have noticed more of those people leaving the city entirely to become full-time residents here. I asked Julie if she was experiencing the same situation. Were the new full-time families with school-aged children enrolling them in her school, a school that may have had a different approach from that which the new residents had known in the city? I had been in the classroom for the morning and had

seen or heard about some of the professional people who were giving their time at the school. Her response surprised me: "A lot of families do like it because most of the families that move out here are coming from private schools where the education is based on the children's abilities and needs, as opposed to strict grade levels that occur in the city's public schools. They find our philosophy of education very similar to what they have been experiencing."

As I personally feel that a multicultural class is an asset, I was pleased to hear that besides mixing the ages, there was also a mixing of socio-economic classes of children. If some of the new residents were still opting for private education for their first to third graders, I felt they were missing out in giving their children an experience that would be hard to duplicate in private school. We quickly moved on in our conversation to the more important reasons for why a multiage concept makes for a successful school. "We are together for three years which translates to a much closer relationship," Julie commented. "I look at them more as 'my children,' sort of a mother-child relationship as opposed to a teacher-student relationship. You may get some people who say, 'that is not the way it should be in education,' but when you are teaching in this kind of environment, I think it is okay. The children need to feel comfortable with you and the school because they are with both of you for three years. And by feeling comfortable they can open up to you so you can discover what is going on in their little minds. As our relationships grow, I develop an ability to read their faces and know by the color of their skin if they are not feeling well or by facial expressions if they are fibbing to me. That is the personal side." Our conversation turned to what I had concentrated my photography on in the morning, the grouping of different ages.

"We work on how to function in a cooperative group during the first few weeks of the year. That established, we proceed from there. Cooperative learning groups are always mixed with the group leader being a third grader and a mix of first, second, and third graders. They have jobs they have to do in the morning and at the end of the day with each other. If they have a problem, they are expected to try and work it out with each other. If the group leader can't solve it among the group then they come to me or any other adult assisting me. If I am busy with a first- or second-grade group and another group needs help, I can sometimes send an older student to help out the group that is having trouble. It is like having several extra little teachers in the classroom at the same time. Other times I'll take a second-grade group to a first-grade reading group to show how well they are reading. It boosts the self-esteem of the first graders, making them feel on the top of the world. It also impresses the second graders and motivates them to stay ahead of those little dynamos."

Seeing how well this school ran impressed me, as had all the others I visited. I felt that Wainscott, having just three grades, had something that approximated the trends of alternative methods of teaching taking place around the country. In certain traditional consolidated schools the educational process of the early grades was being changed to reflect a similar situation as in one-room schools. The prevailing two concepts, one called multi-age (classes with two to three different age levels in them) and the other called looping (where a teacher stays with students for two to three years), were being seen by some sections of the educational community as a better solution to teaching the early grades than having graded classes with a different teacher every year. This was definitely akin to what I had observed in the six schools I visited. Thanks to Judy Jipson at Isle au Haut, I was introduced to Jim Grant, one of the United States' premiere advocates and spokesmen for multi-aging and looping.

Jim Grant has been in the education field since 1967 when he first started teaching in a small school in Dublin, New Hampshire. He is now part of the Society for Developmental Education. He has appeared on the Today show explaining looping, and Phil Donahue and MSNBC talking about school readiness. He started to get interested in looping and multi-age education in the 1970s and began advocating the concepts seriously in the late 1980s. As he told me, "I didn't invent the concepts, they first showed up in this country in a Department of Agriculture pamphlet in 1913. What I did was popularize and spread the concept, hoping to legitimize it as a very viable alternative to standard classes." The benefits from the two concepts were exemplified in all the six one-room schools I mentioned in this chapter. Each teacher got to know the students and their parents better, which allowed for more cooperation between classmates and for learning of the material to proceed faster through mentoring by older students. It also instilled a sense of togetherness in the schoolroom. Jim explained that schools adopt these curriculums enthusiastically but also lose them as new administrators and teachers come into the system not knowing the benefits that had taken place during their practice. "Where they seem to do best is in the suburbs and in the rural areas," said Jim. I understood the rural areas because low enrollment would make multi-aging and looping attractive, but why suburbia? I asked Jim. "The higher the level of parents' education the more they value long-term relationships." That was what Julie had

alluded to with the new families coming to Wainscott from the New York City area, looking for schools for their children.

When I first started this project, I knew nothing of all this. My education began as soon as I started to read books and to interview former students about their one-room schoolhouse experiences. But my most profound learning experience was watching with my own eyes and hearing with my own ears what was happening in these six schools. It was like going back in time, even though computers were lining one side of each school I visited. There was no special show for me. Kids of that age lack pretension, and the teachers were too busy to make anything up. It was a bit old-fashioned, but in a good way, something that the parents of school children would like to see more of. Towards the end of our talk, Jim brought up the tragic events at Columbine High School. He said, "After Columbine, there was a tremendous catapulting of ideas looking at the value of small school units. They were looking to get back to positive relationships. Relationships like what existed in one-room schools, where there was deep caring about each other. Where, in the winter, the older [children] would help get the younger [ones] dressed for recess, where they would help each other out scholastically, where it was like family with deep caring about each other." We both agreed that there is wonderful education taking place in big schools, but it would be nice if we could foster such community in today's classrooms. That was, and is, where the one-room schools excelled.

WAINSCOTT COMMON SCHOOL, WAINSCOTT, NEW YORK.
Reading and assignments with teacher Julie Medler (top row) and part-time teacher Dorry Silvey (bottom row).

WAINSCOTT COMMON SCHOOL, WAINSCOTT, NEW YORK.
This school was founded in 1730.

Bibliography

American education is an immense topic. Listed below are books I found most helpful in navigating through general educational history and specifically the one-room schoolhouse.

Robert Freeman Butts and Lawrence A. Cremin, A History of Education in American Culture
(Holt, Rinehart and Winston, 1953)

Daniel Calhoun, The Educating of Americans: A Documentary History
(Houghton Mifflin Company, 1969)

Andrew Gulliford, America's Country Schools
(The Preservation Press, 1984)

Warren A. Henke and Everett C. Albers, The Legacy of North Dakota's Country Schools
(The North Dakota Humanities Council, Inc., 1998)

Eric Sloane, The Little Red Schoolhouse
(Doubleday & Company, Inc., 1972)

Michele R. Webb (editor), My Folks and the One-Room Schoolhouse
(Capper Press, 1993)

Acknowledgments

I would like to give thanks to everyone who helped me with this project: starting with family members, my wife, Elaine, who is the backbone of all my endeavors, my nieces Kate and Karen Archey for research, and my daughter Jennifer for early proofreading; old friends that always come through, David Larkin and Wendell Garrett; the crew at Universe that believed in this book, Charles Miers, Jane Ginsberg, and Terence Maikels; Verlyn Klinkenborg, for his beautifully written and poignant essay; Claudia Brandenburg, for her imaginative design; my agent, Sheryl Shade; my proofreader, Sara Dulaney; and Gloria Morse, who helped with her historical knowledge. I would also like to thank the state historical offices for their assistance and time, in alphabetical order by state: Alabama, Keri Renee Coumanis; Arizona, William Collins; Arkansas, Mark Christ; California, Joseph McDole; Colorado, Suzanne Doggett; Delaware, Robin K. Bodo; Florida, Janet Snyder Matthews, Ph.D; Georgia, Kenneth H. Thomas, Jr.; Illinois, Tracy A. Sculle; Kansas, Sara J. Keckeisen; Kentucky, Bill Macintire; Louisiana, Pat Duncan; Maine, Christi A. Mitchell; Maryland, Thomas A. Reinhart; Michigan, Laura Ashlee; Minnesota, Steve Nielsen; Mississippi, Jennifer Baughn; Montana, Jeff Patridge; Nebraska, David Murphy; Nevada, Mella Harmon; New Jersey, Bradley M. Campbell; New Mexico, Kenneth H. W. Earle; North Carolina, Michael T. Southern; North Dakota, Susan Dingle; Oklahoma, Jim Gabbert; Oregon, Michelle L. Dennis; South Dakota, Marvene Riis; Texas, Bob Brinkman; Utah, Roger Roper; Vermont, Suzanne C. Jamele; Virginia, Christina M. Wiles; Wisconsin, Joe DeRose; Wyoming, Yvonne Chalifour and Carl Hallberg. And finally, I am grateful to those whose names or images appear in the book. Their willingness to talk to me and be photographed is what really made this book successful.